Well-being

Key Concepts in Philosophy

Well-Being

Ben Bradley

polity

First published in 2015 by Polity Press

Polity Press
65 Bridge Street
Cambridge CB2 1UR, UK

Polity Press
350 Main Street
Malden, MA 02148, USA

ISBN-13: 978-0-7456-6272-5
ISBN-13: 978-0-7456-6273-2(pb)

A catalogue record for this book is available from the British Library.

Library of Congress Cataloging-in-Publication Data

Bradley, Ben, 1971-
  Well-being / Ben Bradley.
    pages cm
  Includes bibliographical references and index.
  ISBN 978-0-7456-6272-5 (hardback : alk. paper) – ISBN 978-0-7456-6273-2
(pbk. : alk. paper) 1. Happiness. 2. Well-being. I. Title.
  BJ1481.B68 2015
  170–dc23
                                      2014049453

Typeset in 10.5 on 12 pt Sabon
by Toppan Best-set Premedia Limited

For further information on Polity, visit our website:
politybooks.com

Contents

Preface

Well-being has always been a central notion in moral and
political philosophy. It plays a role in determining the rightness of actions. Utilitarians claim that morality is entirely
based on well-being – that what we ought to do is make
people as well-off as possible. Deontologists claim that we
have a strict duty not to cause harm; harming someone
seems to involve making that person worse off. Well-being
also plays an important role in theories of justice; when a
hero lives a miserable life, or a villain prospers, we find this
unjust. And prudence seems primarily concerned with well-
being too; to be prudent is just to do what makes one better
off. Well-being is also important outside philosophy. It is
what some "welfare economists" are talking about when they
declare that governments should be promoting well-being
rather than GDP; it is what family courts are talking about
when they make a decision that is alleged to be in the "best
interests" of a child.

The central questions of the book are the following: is
there such a thing as well-being, and if so, what is it? What
constitutes well-being – pleasure, desire satisfaction, knowledge, virtue, achievement, some combination of these, or
something else? What is the importance of well-being for
moral theory, political theory, and public policy? The main
point of this book is not to advocate for a particular answer
to any of these questions, but to give each view a fair shake

and give the reader a feel for the dialectical situation and what is important. After reading this book, one should be prepared to delve more deeply into current academic debates on well-being and should have better perspective on public policy discussions where well-being is an issue.

I have discussed the issues in this book with many people on many occasions. Here are just a few of the folks with whom I have had helpful conversations, or from whom I have received useful comments: Matt Adler, Anna Alexandrova, Gustaf Arrhenius, Krister Bykvist, Steve Campbell, Jeremy Dickinson, Dale Dorsey, Julia Driver, Kirsten Egerstrom, Fred Feldman, Dan Haybron, Chris Heathwood, Hallie Liberto, Eden Lin, Richard Lucas, Amy Massoud, Dale Miller, Dave Sobel, Roy Sorensen (who informed me about Angelman's Syndrome, see ch. 2), Valerie Tiberius, and Travis Timmerman. Special thanks to my research assistant Amy Massoud, who supplied me with detailed reports on recent empirical studies of well-being; to David Sobel and Jeremy Dickinson who commented on drafts of the entire manuscript; to two anonymous referees for very helpful suggestions; and to Pascal Porcheron and Emma Hutchinson at Polity for their patience, encouragement, and guidance.

1
The Concept of Well-Being

1.1 Identifying the Concept

If you go into a bookstore and look at some books in the self-improvement section, you will find some advice about how to make yourself better-off. You'll probably be advised to have some good friends, find some activities or hobbies that you enjoy, eat healthy food, get some regular exercise, reduce the amount of stress in your life, and perhaps join a church or synagogue. For example, in a recent bestselling book, *Wellbeing: The Five Essential Elements*, Tom Rath and James Harter claim that there are five components to well-being: Career Wellbeing, Social Wellbeing, Financial Wellbeing, Physical Wellbeing, and Community Wellbeing (Rath and Harter 2010). This all seems very commonsensical. If someone is healthy and rich, has lots of friends and a good job, and is respected in her community, we will probably regard her as well-off.

But suppose our rich, healthy, popular person is also miserable. She doesn't like her friends and finds her job meaningless. Would we still regard her as well-off? Perhaps not. This should lead us to ask why we care about things like money, health, friends, and a job. What is so good about these things? We want these things only because having them seems to *lead to* being better-off. What a philosopher wants to understand is not just what leads to being better-off, but *what it is* to be better-off. Just what is it that being rich, healthy, employed, and popular allegedly leads to?

Answering this question might be of some practical use. For instance, it might help us determine what to do when different books give us different advice about how to be well-off. Knowing what well-being is might help us to see that one of the books is utilizing a mistaken view about well-being. For example, we might discover that in fact, having lots of money does not lead to well-being at all. But the main purpose of this book is not to evaluate self-help books or to make you better-off. The purpose of this book is to investigate abstract philosophical questions about well-being. Answering these questions might, in the end, not be very useful when it comes to actually being better-off. With luck, though, we will have a better understanding of what it is we are looking for when we try to improve our lives or the lives of others. On some views about well-being, such understanding is itself something that makes us better-off.

There are two main things we want to know. (1) What are we talking about when we talk about well-being? In other words, what do we *mean* by "well-being"? This is a *conceptual question* about well-being. (2) What features does a person's life need to have in order for the person to be well-off? That is, what are the ultimate *determinants* of well-being? This is a *substantial question* about well-being. It is important to distinguish between these questions.

An example might be helpful here. Johnny is six years old. He has never heard of the idea of a "syllable." He hears some older students talking about syllables and talking about how many syllables are in various words. He notices that longer words seem to have more syllables. At that point he can often correctly guess how many syllables are in a word; but he does not yet possess the concept of a syllable. He knows some things: that syllables are related to words in some way, and that longer words usually have more than shorter ones. But more than this is required to have the concept of a syllable. Then someone explains to him how to figure out how many syllables are in a word: "ba-na-na: three syllables." Johnny thus acquires the concept of a syllable. He no longer has to guess how many syllables are in a word; he knows. He might not yet be able to offer a correct *definition* of the word "syllable," but this is not required in order to possess the concept. Now that he has the concept, he can understand what people are talking about when they talk about syllables, can ask meaningful questions, and can engage in disagreements about syllables. For example, he might wonder whether all syllables have a vowel. Learning the answer to that question will not alter his grasp of the concept of a syllable; he knows perfectly well what a syllable is, he just doesn't have complete knowledge of how the concept applies. In the case of well-being, we should first be sure that all parties to the discussion mean the same thing when they say "well-being." Then we can have meaningful disagreements about whether money increases well-being or not, and ask meaningful questions about what the constituents of well-being are.

1.2   Well-Being and Happiness

If you ask someone why they want money, or a job, or to be healthy, they might say it is because those things lead to *happiness*. Thus we might think that well-being should be identified with happiness. But what is happiness? There are at least two ways we might understand what happiness is.

We might take happiness to be a sort of feeling, mood, or experience one has. Perhaps I am happy when I am feeling pleasure; or perhaps I am happy when I am in a good mood. Suppose happiness is something like this; call it "experiential happiness." On the proposal in question, well-being is to be identified with experiential happiness. This way of understanding well-being has some nice features. Everyone knows what it is like to feel good; so everyone can understand what well-being is. And feeling good, or being in a good mood, does seem like something that is important to us.

But there is a problem with this way of understanding well-being. Many philosophers deny that experiential happiness is sufficient for well-being. They say that although you might think you are well-off if you are enjoying yourself, genuine well-being requires something else in addition to having certain experiences (as we will see in chapter 2). Perhaps those philosophers are wrong to say such a thing. But it seems overblown to say that they are *misidentifying the concept* of well-being. If that is so, then we cannot simply identify the concept of well-being with the concept of experiential happiness. While hedonists believe that experiential happiness is necessary and sufficient for being well-off, we do not want to make this a matter of *definition*. It is a claim that needs to be *argued for*, not settled by defining terms in a certain way. If we just stipulate that well-being means happiness, then those other philosophers will just say that they are interested in some other thing – call it well-being* – rather than well-being. All that we accomplish by giving a contentious definition of well-being is to change the venue of debate from the question of whether happiness is the sole component of well-being to the question of whether we should care about well-being or well-being*.

We might understand happiness in a broader sense. We could agree that someone could have good experiences and not be well-off, but also say that such a person would not truly be happy. Happiness, on this view, is more than having certain experiences; to be happy is to *flourish*. (See chapter 4 for more on "flourishing" views of well-being.) Unfortunately, to identify the concept of well-being with the concept of flourishing does not help us much in getting a grasp on the concept of well-being. All we are doing is giving another name, "flourishing," to the thing we are trying to get a grip on.

The trick in identifying the concept of well-being is to do two things at once. (1) Say something so general about well-being that everyone can agree, "yes, that's what I mean when I'm talking about well-being!" (2) Say something informative enough to help us pick out well-being and distinguish it from other concepts. Identifying the concept of well-being with the concept of experiential happiness fails (1). Identifying it with the concept of flourishing fails (2).[1]

---

[1] We might want to say something more specific about flourishing, so that our definition would be more informative. So, for example, we might define flourishing in terms of fulfilling the function of one's kind (see chapter 4). But then our definition would be too specific, and we would have exactly the same problem we had when defining well-being in terms of happiness.

1.3   Well-Being and Goodness

It is important to distinguish between well-being, which is a notion of goodness "for" an individual, and intrinsic goodness, which people sometimes call "just plain" goodness or goodness "*simpliciter*." When we say that something is intrinsically good, we are saying that it is good *in itself* – it makes the world a better place just by being what it is (rather than by causing some other good things to happen). We are not saying that it is good *for* anyone or anything (though it might be that also) – it is just good.

Here is a way to distinguish well-being from just-plain-goodness. Imagine a universe that has no people in it. It contains beautiful sunsets, landscapes, rock formations and such, but not a single conscious being. You might think that such a world would be good – better than no universe at all, and better than an ugly universe (Moore 1903: 83–4). But it wouldn't be good *for* anyone, because there would be no conscious beings there. There would be no well-being at all. This is controversial, of course; you might think a beautiful world would be good only if there were people there to enjoy the beauty. But it is not *conceptually* confused to say that a beautiful world with nobody in it would be a good world. It makes sense to say this, and we understand what is being said when someone says it. So our concept of intrinsic goodness is not the same as our concept of well-being.

Another example that illustrates the difference between goodness and well-being involves what Derek Parfit called the "Non-Identity Problem" (Parfit 1984: ch. 16). Suppose someone is trying to decide whether to conceive a child. She knows if she conceives now, the child who develops will have a genetic condition that will cause him significant pain; his life will still be good for him and well worth living, but it will have this pain in it too. If she waits three months to conceive, the child who develops will have a very similar life but will not have that painful condition. Suppose she conceives now despite all this knowledge. That seems like it makes things worse than if she had waited. But it is not worse for any actual person. If she had waited to conceive, the child who developed would be a different child. Her actual child would not have existed at all, so he would not have been better-off if she had waited. The child she would have had if she had waited does not exist, so he is not worse off either. Thus one situation can be *worse* than another without being *worse for* anyone. This shows that the "just plain goodness" of an outcome is not the same as its goodness for someone. Given that we have two distinct concepts, intrinsic goodness and well-being, we might want to define one in terms of the other. We might say that for some fact to be *good for me* is just for it to be (i) intrinsically good and (ii) about me (Moore 1903: 98–9). Suppose I experience some happiness. My experiencing happiness is intrinsically good; a world with me experiencing happiness is, other things equal, a better world than a world without me experiencing happiness. The fact *that I am happy* is about me; it essentially involves me; I am part of that fact. Thus, according to the proposed definition, my experiencing happiness is good for me.

A nice feature of this definition is that it connects two important value concepts, well-being and intrinsic goodness, by definition. When we have two concepts that are closely related, it is nice to be able to define one in terms of the other rather than having completely distinct concepts. Having such a definitional connection between well-being and goodness would explain *why* well-being is good: part of *what it means* to say that something is good for someone is to say that it is good. But the proposed definition faces serious problems, because it seems possible for there to be facts that are intrinsically good, and about a person, without being good for that person. Suppose justice is intrinsically good, so that it is intrinsically good when someone gets what she deserves. And suppose Joan deserves some pain in virtue of her wicked deeds. Joan's getting pain would be intrinsically good – it would make the world better, other things equal – but it would still not be good for Joan. In fact, from the standpoint of justice, the *whole point* of her suffering the pain, the *reason* it is better that she suffers, is that it would be bad for her. Again, it is controversial whether justice so understood is intrinsically good. But as in the case of beauty, it at least seems conceptually coherent to say that justice is intrinsically good, whether it in fact is good or not. There is no conceptual incoherence in saying that it is intrinsically good when someone gets what she deserves. Since we are investigating conceptual relations between well-being and other concepts, this is sufficient to show that the proposed definition of well-being in terms of goodness cannot be true.

1.4 Well-Being and Caring

We might instead attempt to define well-being by appeal to what we want or care about. The "crib test" offers a way to get a handle on the concept of well-being (Feldman 2004: 9–10). To perform this test, you imagine your new-born child in its crib, and imagine what you would want for that child. If you would want your child's life to have certain elements, then you must think those elements promote the child's well-being. If we were to use a test like this as the basis for a definition of well-being, we might say that someone is well-off when she has the kind of life that someone who cared for her would or should want her to have (Darwall 2004).

This definition seems better than happiness-based definitions. It is very general – people might have very different ideas about what promotes well-being, yet agree that the things that promote well-being are things that they want someone's life to have if they care about that person. And it is, to some degree, informative and useful. It posits a connection between well-being and caring. We already know what it is to care about someone, so we can use that knowledge to understand the nature of well-being.

However, sometimes we want people we care about to have a certain kind of life even though we know that life is not best for them. For example, we might want someone we care about to be honest and generous, or to accomplish something meaningful with her life, even though this might sometimes lead her to sacrifice her own welfare. The problem is that well-being is not the *only* thing we care about when we care about our loved ones. So the caring account makes well-being too expansive.

We might add a clause to the definition to get around this problem. We could say that someone is well-off when she has the kind of life that someone who cared about her would want for her, *for her own sake* (Darwall 2004). There are certain things we want for our loved ones even though they might not increase their well-being, such as virtue and achievement, but we don't necessarily want those things for our loved ones' *sakes*. We might want them for our own sake, or for the sake of others, or because it would make the universe better; in these cases, the things we want are not components of the person's well-being. But adding this clause makes our definition uninformative. When we say we want something for someone's sake, we just mean we want it for the sake of her well-being. It is not very helpful to say that well-being is what we want for someone when we care about her well-being.

It does seem true that well-being is *among* the things we want, or ought to want, for someone we care about. What's more, it is something we want *intrinsically* for that person – that is, we just want that person to have it, even if it does not lead to any other things we care about for her. In this respect, it is very unlike money or a job; we usually want those we care about to have money or a job, but only in virtue of what having those things leads to. But we might also want that person to be virtuous even if being virtuous fails to lead to any other good things for her; and we might want this even if we don't think being virtuous promotes her well-being. So we cannot simply identify a person's well-being with what a loved one wants for her, but we can perhaps use this as a test: if there is something that we have absolutely no reason to want for someone we care about, then it is *not* a component of well-being.

Perhaps these attempted definitions of well-being point us in the direction of the concept we are trying to grasp. We need not take the failure to define a concept as reason not to use it; some concepts are basic and undefinable. Well-being may be one of those concepts. It is useful to see its connections to concepts like happiness, goodness, and caring, even if it cannot be defined in terms of them. Well-being is happiness, in the broadest sense of "happiness" – it is flourishing. Well-being is something that, normally, is good in itself and makes the universe better. It is one of the most important things we want for those we care about.

1.5   The Subjects of Well-Being

Philosophical discussions of well-being usually focus on *human* well-being. This makes sense, since the discussions are carried out by humans, and we humans tend to care most about ourselves and other humans. This book will generally focus on human well-being too, since it attempts to give the reader a sense of the philosophical landscape concerning well-being, which has been human-centered. But it would be a mistake to suppose that only humans have a well-being. It seems clear that at least some non-humans have a welfare. If you own a dog or a cat, you almost certainly believe that your pet can be benefited or harmed. It will be worthwhile to think about how the various theories of well-being can be applied to non-human animals.

When we realize that non-humans can be well-off, we might then wonder how far the concept of well-being can extend. Suppose you own a piano. You might have been told to keep the piano away from the colder or warmer areas of the house, since extreme temperatures can be bad for the piano. Suppose you own a car. You probably get its oil changed regularly, because this is good for the car. So some things are good or bad for pianos and cars. Does it follow that pianos and cars have a welfare? That seems unlikely. Talk about what is good for a car or a piano seems meta-phorical, or shorthand for something else. What's "good for a car" or "good for a piano" is what helps it continue to operate as you want it to. Cars and pianos are artifacts that have no importance apart from our interests in their function-ing; they are unlike people and dogs in that respect.

Dogs really do have well-being, and cars do not; but what makes this so? Dogs are *sentient*, like humans; that is, they have conscious mental lives. Perhaps genuine well-being is something that can be had only by sentient beings. But we might wonder about this. What about, for example, an eco-system? Introduction of an alien species into an ecosystem can be bad for the ecosystem. Saying that it is bad for the ecosystem does not just mean that it keeps the ecosystem from operating in the way we want it to; ecosystems are not artifacts, like pianos and cars. Does that mean ecosystems have genuine well-being, in the sense that people do? What about trees? Sunlight and water are good for trees; some beetles and fungi are bad for them. So do trees have a well-being? Sometimes when we say that something is well-off, we just mean that it is *healthy*. Ecosystems and trees have a well-being in this sense: they can be healthy or unhealthy. But it doesn't follow that trees and ecosystems have well-being in the robust way that humans and dogs do; a human can be healthy but still not be well-off in this more robust way. Given most theories of well-being that we will discuss (with the possible exception of "perfectionist" theories discussed in chapter 4), trees and ecosystems will not turn out to be candidates for having genuine well-being, since they have no mental life.

There is another class of beings that poses interesting questions: beings that are not alive, but are sentient. Perhaps there are no such beings at present, but in the future we might develop a computer that is sentient but not alive. Perhaps such a computer would have genuine well-being. This seems more plausible if we imagine that it can feel emotions – for example, if it can enjoy or be pained by things. On some leading theories of well-being, emotional computers would have genuine well-being of the sort that humans have.

For now, let us be fairly open-minded about what sorts of things can have genuine well-being. Let us say that the kind of well-being we will focus on is a kind of well-being that is definitely had by living, sentient beings such as humans and dogs, is definitely not had by objects that are not alive or sentient (like cars), and might or might not be had by non-sentient but living things like trees and by sentient but non-living things like emotional computers.

1.6   Intrinsic and Instrumental Value

Let us suppose that we have said enough to ensure that you and I are picking out the same concept of well-being: that you and I sufficiently share an understanding of the type of benefit that can happen to people and dogs but probably not to trees and certainly not to cars. Thus, we are supposing, we are like the child who grasps the same concept of syllable that her classmates are using. Now we can meaningfully agree or disagree with each other, secure in the assumption that we are talking about the same thing and not just talking past each other.

We now need to make an important conceptual distinction that will help us categorize the various goods that we have been discussing. There are some things that make us better-off by *causing* us to be well-off. As mentioned above, having money, being healthy, having a job, and having friends are all things that tend to cause people to be better-off than they would be otherwise (though of course not always!). These things are *instrumentally* good for us. There are other things that make us better-off just by being part of our lives, even if they do not cause us to be better-off. These are the *constituents* of well-being, or the things that are *intrinsically* good for us. The most interesting philosophical problem about well-being is determining what those constituents are: what things are intrinsically good for us? Pleasure is one obvious candidate, but there are many others, including knowledge, virtue, friendship, achievement, meaning, fulfilling one's desires, and developing one's talents. In the next few chapters we will examine these possibilities. In chapter 6 we will briefly discuss the other question: what things are instrumentally good for us? This is a question that philosophers are less well suited to answer, so we will look at how psychologists attempt to answer it.

1.7 Further Reading

For some recent discussions of the conceptual distinction between well-being and happiness, see Wayne Davis, "Pleasure and Happiness" (Davis 1981), Dan Haybron, "Happiness and Pleasure" (Haybron 2001), and ch. 2 of Haybron's *The Pursuit of Unhappiness* (Haybron 2008). Stephen Darwall defends an analysis of well-being in terms of caring in *Welfare and Rational Care* (Darwall 2004). G.E. Moore famously questions the very notion of "goodness for" in section 59 of *Principia Ethica* (Moore 1903). Moore's ultimate target there is egoism, or the view that each person ought to do what is best for him or her; see Crisp (2013) for discussion of Moore's argument. Kris McDaniel defends an analysis of well-being in terms of intrinsic goodness, along lines Moore might have endorsed, in "A Moorean View of the Value of Lives" (McDaniel 2014). For further criticism of the notion of well-being, see chapter 3 of T.M. Scanlon's *What We Owe to Each Other* (Scanlon 1998). See Connie Rosati's "Personal Good" (2006) and Part Two of Richard Kraut's *What Is Good and Why* (2007) for discussion of the nature of the "good for" relation.

2
Hedonism

Hedonists believe that *pleasure and pain* are the only fundamental components of well-being. In discussing hedonism,
the first question to ask is: what are pleasure and pain? We
will focus on the nature of pleasure.

2.1 What Pleasure Is

Broadly speaking, there are two views about the nature of
pleasure. On one view, pleasure is a certain distinctive kind
of *feeling*. Just as there are feelings of coldness or warmth,
pressure, nausea, and the taste of strawberries, there is also
the feeling of pleasure itself. This feeling might be caused by
other feelings. For example, eating strawberries might cause
one to have the taste of strawberries, and this in turn might
cause one to have the feeling of pleasure itself. But the feeling
of pleasure is not the same thing as the taste of strawberries.
It is a distinct feeling. The very same feeling of pleasure is
caused by many different kinds of experiences, such as the
pressure of a massage, or the warmth of the sun. Call this the
"distinctive feeling view."
  We might doubt the distinctive feeling view in light of the
fact that it is difficult to pin down what the feeling of pleasure
would be. You may find it implausible that there is a single

distinct feeling that you have when you enjoy eating a straw-berry and when you enjoy the sun's warmth. What do those sensations have in common? Furthermore, consider how it feels to enjoy having completed a difficult puzzle. Does this feel anything like eating a strawberry? *Is there even a way it feels at all?* If you don't think so, then you cannot accept the distinctive feeling view.

Suppose pleasure is not a distinctive feeling – then what is it? According to Henry Sidgwick, pleasures are feelings that we want to continue (Sidgwick 1907: 42–3). Thus if I am having the pleasant experience of eating a strawberry, there are certain taste sensations that I want to continue – those sensations are themselves pleasures. Those sensations do not feel the same as the sensations of warmth I get from the sun when I am enjoying being outside. What they have in common is that I want both to continue – but I can want two sensations to continue even though they feel completely different from one another. Call this view the "**desire view**" of pleasure.

On another view, pleasure is not a feeling at all. Rather, it is an *attitude*. Attitudes include such things as desires, beliefs, hopes, and fears. When one has a belief, there is nothing it feels like to have that belief. Beliefs are mental states that are about something. So, for example, I believe that it is sunny outside. My belief is about the weather – in particular it is about the proposition that *it is sunny*. You can't have a belief that isn't a belief about something. Belief is, in this way, unlike the feeling of warmth. The sun might *cause* you to feel warm, but your feeling of warmth is not *about* the sun. On the attitudinal view of pleasure, when you are pleased, there is always something you are pleased about. You might be pleased that you are meeting someone you've wanted to meet, or that your team is winning the game. You might be pleased that you are having a feeling of warmth. In all these cases, pleasure is an attitude directed at some fact – the fact that you are meeting someone, or that you are feeling warm. Call this the "**attitudinal view**."

We do not need to decide which of these three views about pleasure is true. But the distinction will come in handy as we examine different versions of hedonism.

It will be helpful to remind ourselves of some very common assumptions we tend to make about pleasure and pain. One assumption is that pleasures and pains come in different intensities and durations. Obviously, some pleasures last longer than others. Some pleasures are also more intense than others. The pleasure a child gets on a rollercoaster is an intense, but short-lived, pleasure. The pleasure you get when reading an enjoyable book is not very intense, but it might last a very long time. It is difficult, in practice, to determine exactly how intense or how long-lasting a pleasure is. Maybe this would involve hooking up some scientific machinery to your brain. That might itself interfere with the experience of pleasure. In practice, we have to rely on what our experiences tell us about how intense an experience of pleasure is. The intensity and duration of a pleasure determine how much pleasure there is in that experience of pleasure. The more intense, or the more long-lasting, a pleasure is, the more pleasure there is in it.

Note, however, that the intensity of a pleasure should not be confused with the intensity of the experience that causes the pleasure, or the intensity of the experience that the pleasure is about. One might have a very intense feeling of heat upon eating some very hot food, but the feeling of pleasure does not increase as the feeling of heat increases. The same goes for duration. When you get pleasure from eating a donut, the pleasant feelings and the taste sensations overlap for a time; but as you keep eating the donuts, you get tired of the taste, and eventually the pleasant feelings go away even as you continue stuffing yourself full of donuts and receiving donut taste sensations.

Another very natural thought we tend to have is that pleasures and pains can be weighed against one another. Pleasure and pain are distinct feelings or attitudes. The hedonist thinks that pleasures are intrinsically good and pains are intrinsically bad. So there must be some amount of pleasure that counterbalances some amount of pain, such that if you enjoyed that amount of pleasure but also suffered that amount of pain, the net result for you would be neither good nor bad on the whole. But what are these amounts of pleasure and pain? That is a question that hedonists have a difficult time answering. Let us suppose that there is a unit of pleasure, the *hedon*, and a unit of pain, the *dolor*. One hedon and one dolor cancel each other out. The units of pleasure and pain are arbitrary, like the choice of measuring distance in feet or meters. But once we choose our hedon, we must then be careful in our choice of the dolor. If one hedon is the amount of pleasure received from a few minutes of enjoying the warmth of the sun, then one dolor should not be the amount of pain suffered from a kidney stone attack. These do not balance each other out. There is more pain in the kidney stone attack than there is pleasure in the few minutes of warmth.

2.2   Simple Hedonism

Now that we have some idea of what pleasure and pain are, let us carefully state the theory. When we state a theory of well-being, we need to make sure to identify what exactly it is that is intrinsically good or intrinsically bad for someone. We also need to say what it is that determines *how good* or *how bad* something is for someone. And we need to say how the intrinsically good and bad things determine how well someone's *whole life* goes. (We will focus more on the third question in chapter 6.)

We have assumed that pleasures have an intensity and a duration, and these determine how much pleasure is contained in an experience of pleasure. According to hedonism, what is intrinsically good for someone is an experience of pleasure. *How good* that experience of pleasure is for that person is equal to *the amount of pleasure* in it, or the number of hedons. The same goes for pain, except that it is bad; the intrinsic value of an experience of pain is negative, and it is more negative the more dolors are in it. Finally, to determine how well or badly someone's whole life goes, we just add up the intrinsic values of the pleasures and pains (where, again, the value of pain is negative) contained in that life – or, in other words, we subtract the dolors from the hedons. The higher the number, the better the life. If the number is negative, the person would have been better-off never having come into existence (though her life could still be *worth living* in non-welfare-related ways, such as by being useful to others).

So far we have not given any reasons to take hedonism seriously. Why should we believe hedonism? There are various reasons that might be offered.

Psychological Hedonism

Some have claimed that basic facts about human psychology show that hedonism must be true. John Stuart Mill argues in the following way:

> The utilitarian doctrine is that happiness is desirable, and the only thing desirable, as an end; all other things being only desirable as a means to that end. What ought to be required of this doctrine, what conditions is it requisite that the doctrine should fulfill, to make good its claim to be believed? The only proof capable of being given that an object is visible is that people actually see it. The only proof that a sound is audible is that people hear it; and so of the other sources of our experience. In like manner, I apprehend, the sole evidence it is possible to produce that anything is desirable is that people do actually desire it. (Mill 1861: 44)

Bear in mind that Mill holds a hedonistic view of happiness: "by happiness is intended pleasure and the absence of pain" (Mill 1861: 10). Since people do in fact desire their own happiness, Mill takes himself to have shown "that happiness is a good, that each person's happiness is a good to that person" (1861: 45). But as Mill himself admits, this does not show that hedonism is true. Hedonism is the view that pleasure is the *only* thing that is intrinsically good for us. So if we ever desire anything other than pleasure, Mill's reasoning would also seem to prove that something other than pleasure is intrinsically good for us, and therefore that hedonism is false.

Do we ever desire anything other than pleasure? Mill himself thought that we do desire some things other than pleasure or happiness. (He also thought that those things then somehow become "part" of happiness (Mill 1861: 46), so his view on these matters is less than clear; I won't attempt to determine here what is the best interpretation of Mill's views on well-being.) But some have argued that we in fact desire only happiness. Jeremy Bentham colorfully pronounces this at the beginning of his "Introduction to the Principles of Morals and Legislation":

> Nature has placed mankind under the governance of two sovereign masters, *pain* and *pleasure*. It is for them alone to point out what we ought to do, as well as to determine what we shall do. On the one hand the standard of right and wrong, on the other the chain of causes and effects, are fastened to their throne. They govern us in all we do, in all we say, in all we think: every effort we can make to throw off our subjection, will serve but to demonstrate and confirm it. In words a man may pretend to abjure their empire: but in reality he will remain subject to it all the while. (Bentham 1962 [1789]: 33)

Here Bentham endorses two doctrines: one ethical, one psychological. The ethical doctrine, utilitarianism, we will return to in chapter 7. The psychological doctrine is **psychological hedonism**, which is the view that the only thing that people desire *for itself* is pleasure or to avoid pain. People desire things other than pleasure – for example, people desire to eat food – but they desire these things only because they are a *means* to pleasure or to avoiding pain. Pleasure and pain are the fundamental motivators of our behavior ("it is for them alone...to determine what we shall do"). Psychological hedonism is not a view about what is good or bad for us; it is not a view about well-being. It is a *psychological* theory about why we behave the way we do.

We now have the makings of an argument for hedonism. Suppose that Bentham is right, and psychological hedonism is true: the only thing people desire for itself is pleasure. And suppose that something is intrinsically good for us if and only if we desire it for itself, as Mill seems to be arguing in the passage above. It follows that pleasure is the only thing that is intrinsically good for us.

Unfortunately, this argument is very weak. First, consider Mill's analogy between desirability and visibility. When we say that something is visible, we mean that it *can* be seen. So showing that someone sees something would be a good way to prove that it can be seen, because whatever is actual must be possible. When we say that something is desirable, however, we do not (typically) mean that it can be desired. We mean, rather, that it *ought to be* desired, or is worthy of being desired. And the fact that people desire something gives us no reason at all to think that it is worthy of being desired, any more than the fact that people see something gives us a reason to think that it is worthy of being seen. Some people have seen the movie *Battlefield Earth*, but few of those people would agree that it was worthy of being seen.

Second, psychological hedonism seems false. There appear to be many instances in which someone acts without being motivated by a desire to get pleasure or avoid pain. For example, people often act from a sense of duty. If my friend is sick in the hospital, I might go visit him to cheer him up. I would do this not because I would enjoy it; I find hospitals unpleasant, and would get more enjoyment from doing something else. I would do it because I think I ought to do it. There are more noble examples of this sort of behavior: for example, the soldier who sacrifices his life to save the life of a comrade. This behavior is hard to explain on the supposition that psychological hedonism is true. The psychological hedonist might argue that in these cases, the person who allegedly acts from duty is in fact acting from a desire to avoid the pain he would feel if he failed in his duty. But why should we believe this? There seems no reason other than that the theory tells us so. If psychological hedonism were sufficiently justified, for example by being supported by evidence or experimental data, or by its great explanatory power, then we might have reason to think that in cases where someone seems to be acting from duty or from some other motive, they are really acting from a desire to receive pleasure or avoid pain. But psychological hedonism is not justified in any of those ways. We have no experimental evidence for its truth; it does not seem to have greater explanatory power than alternative theories according to which people can be motivated by duty or by altruistic desires. In light of this, we ought to regard psychological hedonism with skepticism.

So this argument for hedonism does not seem very convincing. That does not mean hedonism is not true; there are other reasons we might give for accepting hedonism. I will give several reasons. None of these amounts to a knockdown argument for hedonism, but perhaps they give us some reason to accept it, depending on whether we can find another theory that is better.

Pleasure, Pain, and Reasons

Well-being provides reasons for action. The fact that some action will make someone worse off provides a reason not to do that action. This seems hard to deny. It also seems hard to deny that pleasure and pain provide reasons for action: the fact that an action will cause someone pain provides a reason not to do that action. Suppose Ned says to Homer, "Could you please move your car? It's on my foot, and it hurts!" And suppose Homer were to reply: "Yes, I can see that you are in pain. And I can see that my car being on your foot is the cause of the pain. But how does that give me any reason to move my car? I just don't see any connection between these things." We would have to assume that Homer is joking, or intentionally being a jerk, or perhaps that Homer is not even a human being, or has somehow reached adulthood without acquiring the concepts of *reason* and *pain*. Suppose Homer then said: "I suppose if pain were bad for you, I would have a reason to move my car; but I don't think pain is bad for you, so I see no such reason." In that case, it seems possible that Homer actually does have the concepts of reason, pain, and well-being. But his behavior is not made any less absurd when we discover that it is based on the view that pain is not bad for Ned. It seems clear that pleasure and pain are *among* the constituents of well-being, and therefore provide reasons for action.

The Possibility of Measurement

Under most circumstances it is fairly easy to tell when someone is experiencing pleasure or pain, and even easier for one to tell that she herself is having such experiences. This suggests that if hedonism were true – if pleasure and pain were not merely *among* the constituents, but were the *sole* constituents, of well-being – there would be some prospect of measuring well-being, even if not very precisely. In chapter 6 we will examine how social scientists have attempted to measure hedonic well-being.

Comparing Goods

Hedonism seems to have other advantages as well. For example, suppose I am wondering whether reading a book or going for a run would be better for me. The hedonist says that the one that would be better for me is the one that would bring about more pleasure for me. If I would enjoy reading more than running, it would be prudent for me to read. So we have a relatively easy way, at least in principle, to compare the values of our options. Suppose, on the other hand, that there were two things that were intrinsically good for us: pleasure and knowledge, for example. Then we would need some way to compare the value of some pleasure with the value of some knowledge. This would be a very difficult task.

Non-Elitism

Hedonism is also not elitist. If someone else enjoys running more than reading, it would be better for that person to run than to read. "To each his own," the hedonist might say, and this seems like an attractive thought. It would be unappealing to say that even though I hate running, and running would have no positive impact on my net hedonic balance, still it would be good for me to run.

The Possibility of Mistakes

Although hedonism is tolerant of differences in taste, it also allows for the possibility of making mistakes. Jerry sees a carton of ice cream and desires to eat the whole thing, and he does; he ends up getting a terrible stomachache afterwards. The hedonist will say that Jerry made a prudential error. He thought eating the whole carton would be the best thing for him to do, but he was wrong. Jerry would probably agree; but hedonism entails that he made a mistake whether he agrees or not. The amount of pain he caused himself rendered his decision imprudent no matter what Jerry thinks about the matter. According to hedonism, the desire for pain (unless it is required to bring a greater pleasure) is irrational, and so at least some masochists are irrational. So are ascetics, or those who eschew pleasure – again, unless eschewing pleasure results in avoiding even greater pain. So a more accurate but less catchy slogan for the hedonist than "to each his own" would be "to each whatever best promotes her total balance of pleasure over pain."

Despite these reasons in favor of hedonism, few philosophers today accept it, at least in the simple form presented here. I now turn to reasons that have been given to reject hedonism.

2.3 Base Pleasures and Quality of Pleasure

Sadly, there are people who get pleasure from hurting other people or animals. Imagine someone who gets intense pleasure from torturing and killing kittens. Imagine that due to lax animal welfare laws, he can get lots of these pleasures without having to worry about being put in jail. He never feels any remorse for any of his actions. According to hedonism, such a person would have a very high welfare level. But we do not think that this person is very well-off.

In reply, the hedonist might accuse the objector of forgetting what it is that we are talking about. If someone gets pleasure from performing immoral actions, *something* is going wrong with the person's life. There is some dimension of evaluation according to which the person is not doing well. But, says the hedonist, it is not the *well-being dimension* of evaluation that is problematic. The pleasure this person gets from performing immoral actions *is* beneficial to that person. In fact, this explains why we find the situation so abhorrent: it is unjust for someone to benefit from his ill deeds. We are not here interested in the question of what makes someone a good person, or what makes for a virtuous life. We are trying to figure out what makes a person better-off. When we are clearly focused on that question, it is not clear that getting pleasure from an immoral source does not make the person better-off.

However, similar objections can be raised that involve subjects getting pleasure from less evil but still not very impressive activities, such as taking drugs, eating pizza, and playing video games. Deriving pleasure from such activities might not be worthless, and might even make your life go better. But would your life go extremely well if these were the only sorts of pleasures you had? You probably do not think so. Of course, the hedonist might agree. He can point out that eating too much pizza will probably make you sick; watching too much TV makes people depressed; drugs are addictive. Furthermore, you might get bored of these activities, and they would stop being pleasant for you. But still: suppose you didn't get bored, or sick, or depressed, or addicted. Could you have a life very high in welfare that consisted only of such activities? Many would say you could not. And most people who have children would not be thrilled at the thought of them living their lives sitting on a couch eating pizza and watching TV, even if any bad consequences could be avoided.

Finally, consider the genetic disorder called Angelman's Syndrome. Those who have AS have severe developmental delays and little or no verbal communicative ability, among other problems; but they also exhibit "frequent laughter/ smiling; apparent happy demeanor."[2] It is hard to be sure, but suppose those with AS really are experiencing pleasure very frequently. Hedonism entails that their lives are going very well. Yet we might find this hard to believe. It is hard to imagine people lamenting the fact that they or their children were not born with AS.

Some hedonists are persuaded that base pleasures are less valuable than other pleasures, but are not led to abandon hedonism. Rather, they formulate more sophisticated versions of hedonism in order to get hedonism to be compatible with the examples.

The most well-known version of a more sophisticated hedonism is Mill's. Mill claims that pleasures can be measured not only by quantity, but by quality. Quality is not the

---

[2] http://www.angelman.org/understanding-as/medical-info/ diagnostic-criteria/

same thing as intensity. It is a separate dimension of evaluation. According to **qualified hedonism**, there are higher and lower quality pleasures; given two pleasures of the same intensity and duration, one might still be more valuable than another. The pleasures of pizza would count as lower-quality pleasures, while the pleasures of listening to opera or performing morally praiseworthy actions would count as higher-quality. Higher-quality pleasures are more valuable than lower-quality pleasures; this could help explain why the life spent pleasantly eating pizza is not such a great life for the person living it.

Henry Sidgwick and G.E. Moore argued that it is incoherent to distinguish pleasures in this way (Sidgwick 1907: 94–5; Moore 1903: 79). Why should it matter, when considering the *intrinsic* value of a pleasure, what *causes* the pleasure? Keeping intensity and duration fixed, the feeling of pleasure itself is the same no matter what causes it, so it should be equally valuable no matter what causes it. If you think it is better to get pleasure from listening to opera than from eating pizza, then you must think that listening to opera is better than eating pizza – but the hedonist cannot say that listening to opera has any intrinsic value at all. Its value is instrumental – it is good for you because it makes you pleased.

But this criticism finds its mark only if we suppose that pleasure is a distinct kind of feeling. Suppose, instead, that we accepted an attitudinal view of pleasure. Being pleased that you are eating pizza and being pleased that you are listening to a beautiful opera are different mental states, and so it is conceivable that they could differ in value even if the intensity and duration of the pleasure were the same (Feldman 2004: 71–8). So let us take qualified hedonism to be the view that (i) attitudinal pleasures are intrinsically good for us and attitudinal pains are intrinsically bad for us; (ii) the value of an attitudinal pleasure is determined by its intensity, duration, and *what the pleasure is taken in*; and (iii) how well someone's life goes is determined by adding up the values of the attitudinal pleasures and pains in it.

(An interesting question: are there also differences in quality of pain? It would be natural to think that if pleasures differ in quality, pains do too. But which pains would count as "higher" or "lower" in quality? I find it difficult to say whether the pain of failing to complete a puzzle is higher or lower in quality than the pain of tennis elbow. I will assume that pains differ only in intensity and duration, not in quality.)

This is an outline of a view, but the obvious question is: what distinguishes higher-quality pleasures from lower-quality pleasures? Here is what Mill says about this:

> If I am asked what I mean by difference of quality in pleasures, or what makes one pleasure more valuable than another, merely as a pleasure, except its being greater in amount, there is but one possible answer. Of two pleasures, if there be one to which all or almost all who have experience of both give a decided preference, irrespective of any feeling of moral obligation to prefer it, that is the more desirable pleasure. If one of the two is, by those who are competently acquainted with both, placed so far above the other that they prefer it, even though knowing it to be attended with a greater amount of discontent, and would not resign it for any quantity of the other pleasure which their nature is capable of, we are justified in ascribing to the preferred enjoyment a superiority in quality so far outweighing quantity as to render it, in comparison, of small account. (1861: 12)

Here Mill seems to be saying that what makes a pleasure a higher-quality pleasure than another is that all or almost all who have experienced both pleasures, the "competent judges" (1861: 15), would prefer it, keeping the amount of pleasure fixed. So, for example, suppose that you could get some pleasure from attending the opera, or the same amount of pleasure from eating pizza. And suppose that all who have enjoyed pizza and the opera would choose the opera in this circumstance. That would show that the opera pleasure is higher quality.

But it is hard to believe that Mill thought that the preference of all or almost all competent judges is what *makes* a pleasure higher quality. This would make distinctions in quality too *extrinsic* to the pleasures. If the competent judges changed some of their preferences and started liking pizza over all else, pizza pleasures would become high quality – thus, if I enjoy a lot of pizza pleasures in my life, my life would go from being mediocre to being excellent just because the competent judges start preferring pizza rather than opera.

How could their judgments *determine* the value of my life? Furthermore, imagine that you are a competent judge whose preferences differ from all the other competent judges. They all strongly prefer peaches to watermelon, but you strongly prefer watermelon to peaches. Should we conclude that your preference is mistaken, and in fact peaches are better for you? The quality of your life must be independent of what happens to be going on with the preferences of others.

It is easier to believe that the preference of the competent judge is *evidence* (if not wholly conclusive evidence) that a pleasure is higher in quality, but that high-quality pleasures have some other feature that makes them high quality and that competent judges would notice and value. Mill tells us what feature high-quality pleasures have in common: they are the ones that involve the "higher faculties" (1861: 12), such as the ability to appreciate art and to act morally, which are not shared by non-human animals (or by most – there are stories of elephants painting and of chimpanzees exhibiting some sort of proto-moral behavior, so we should not be too quick to assume that what we think of as "higher faculties" are exclusive to humanity). Presumably, the *reason* competent judges prefer opera pleasure to pizza pleasure is that opera pleasure involves our higher faculties, while pizza pleasure can be had by any animal that can eat food.

Perhaps this is too simplistic, however. We can think of some kinds of pleasures that involve "higher" faculties but do not seem to be high-quality pleasures. Someone might get pleasure from acting immorally, but non-human animals are not capable of acting immorally; so the pleasures of immorality involve the higher faculties, yet we do not think that such pleasures are more valuable than the pleasures of eating pizza. Other animals cannot play video games, but we don't think that a life spent playing video games is wonderful for a human either.

There are other activities that do not involve higher faculties, but it would seem elitist to say they are lower in quality. For instance, sprinters employ only faculties shared by animals while they are running. (In fact, the Fox TV special *Man vs. Beast* featured a human sprinter racing against a giraffe and a zebra; he beat the giraffe but lost to the zebra.) But does this mean the pleasure people get from running is low-quality pleasure, and that runners would be better-off going to the opera? This would undermine the non-elitism that was part of what made hedonism attractive in the first place.

Another perplexing thing about Mill's competent judges test is that there are certain activities that most people simply would never do, and only someone already inclined to enjoy that activity would be likely to do it. Torturing animals might be a good example of this. Most of us are not qualified, on Mill's grounds, to judge whether the pleasure received from torturing an animal is preferable to opera pleasure. Only one who has experienced both types of pleasure is a competent judge, according to Mill. It could well turn out that those who have experienced both types of pleasure tend to prefer the torture pleasures, since only those prone to like torture would ever experience torture pleasures in the first place. The rest of us disqualify ourselves from being competent judges by rightly abstaining from such behaviors. If the animal torturer is the only competent judge and prefers the torture pleasures to opera pleasures, this would make the torture pleasures higher in quality than opera pleasures. This is an unwelcome result.

None of this shows that pleasures do not differ in quality. But it does show that it is not easy to give an account of such differences. Appeals to competent judges and higher faculties seem unlikely to give us an account of what makes something a higher-quality pleasure.

2.4 False Pleasures

Robert Nozick famously described an example that many have thought is fatal for hedonism:

> Suppose there were an experience machine that would give you any experience you desired. Superduper neuropsychologists could stimulate your brain so that you would think and feel you were writing a great novel, or making a friend, or reading an interesting book. All the time you would be floating in a tank, with electrodes attached to your brain. Should you plug into this machine for life, preprogramming your life experiences? (Nozick 1974: 42)

Most people would say that a life on such a machine would not be a wonderful life for the person living it, and would not choose it for themselves or their loved ones. It is not that if you choose the life of the experience machine, you will later on experience great pain as a result of your choice, perhaps by exiting the machine and discovering that you have no life anymore. The claim is that *even if you don't later experience any pain* as a result of being in the machine, you have not benefited greatly by your experiences of pleasure.

Is this a convincing argument against hedonism? There are many reasons one might choose not to enter the experience machine, and not all of those reasons have to do with the effects the machine would have on your well-being. It might be *immoral* to enter the experience machine, since one would be shirking one's duties to family and friends. If you enter the machine, your life will be less excellent along some dimensions: you won't be living a life of achievement, or a fully virtuous life; you'll be abandoning commitments you have made (Kawall 1999). But these reasons do not settle the question of whether your life would be *beneficial* to you if you were in the machine. According to the hedonist, although living in the experience machine would be bad in various ways, it would be excellent along the dimension of well-being. The hedonist thinks that the critic mistakenly infers, from the fact that it would make sense to refuse to enter the machine, that entering the machine would not be beneficial.

Examples involving experience machines are fanciful. This does not mean they are not useful. A theory of well-being needs to give a correct accounting of all the lives we could live, not just actual or realistic ones. But there are plenty of more realistic examples that point to a similar problem for hedonism. Just imagine someone who gets a great deal of enjoyment from his personal and professional life, yet all the while his friends, family, and co-workers are mocking and betraying him behind his back (Nagel 1993: 64). He believes he has fulfilling, valuable relationships with the people in his life, but they do not regard those relationships in the same way he does. Unbeknownst to him, he does not have any real friends at all. This seems like a very sad life for someone to live. The hedonist might claim that what you don't know can't hurt you – as long as he does not find out about the mockery and betrayal, and he is enjoying his life, things are in fact going well for him. To see whether you think this is an adequate response, imagine that he does find out. Now ask yourself: when did things start to go badly for him? When his "friends" were betraying him, or when he found out about the betrayal? Did the discovery of the betrayal *make* things go badly, or was it rather that he *discovered* that things were going badly already?

Just as Mill attempts to formulate a version of hedonism that discounts base or immoral pleasures, we might formulate a version of hedonism that discounts *false* pleasures. According to Fred Feldman's **truth-adjusted hedonism**, pleasures taken in what is true are better for us than pleasures taken in what is false (2004: 112). To formulate truth-adjusted hedonism, let us suppose that the attitudinal view about pleasure is true, and that pleasures have *objects*. While the simple hedonist says that the intrinsic value of a pleasure is determined simply by the number of hedons in it, the truth-adjusted hedonist says that the intrinsic value of pleasure is determined by the number of hedons in it *and the truth-value of the object of the pleasure*. Since pleasures taken in false things are not as good for us as pleasures taken in true things, one who lives in an experience machine or who is secretly betrayed by his friends and family could be worse off than someone whose pleasures are taken in truths, even if the true pleasures are less pleasant than the false ones.

Is this even a form of hedonism? We might think that truth-adjusted hedonism entails that pleasure is not the sole intrinsic good. If I am pleased that I just climbed Mount Everest, and in fact I did just climb Mount Everest, the truth-adjusted hedonist says that this is better for me than if I didn't climb it but merely thought I did (as would be the case if I were in the experience machine having climbing experiences). According to the objection, this must mean that climbing Mount Everest is intrinsically good for me. And that is incompatible with hedonism. If you think it is intrinsically good to climb a mountain, you are not a hedonist, for you think that something other than pleasure is intrinsically good.

But the truth-adjusted hedonist does not say that climbing Mount Everest is intrinsically good. What is intrinsically good is the *pleasure* taken in climbing Mount Everest, when one has done it. Still, we might wonder whether this is in the spirit of hedonism, for it seems to amount to saying that what is intrinsically good is the *combination* of two things: the pleasure taken in climbing Everest and the fact that one has climbed Everest. Only one of those two things is a pleasure. What is intrinsically good for us, according to truth-adjusted hedonism, is the combination of a pleasure and some other fact about the world. Truth-adjusted hedonism is better thought of as a hybrid theory.

2.5 The Intrinsic Values of Non-Pleasures

Even if we think the hedonist can get around the problems of base and false pleasures, we might think hedonism is false. We might even admit that base and false pleasures are good for us, but still think that there are some things other than pleasure that contribute to well-being, such as desire satisfaction, knowledge, achievement, friendship, and virtue. All of these are things that seem to be lacking in large measure from the lives of people who are radically deceived about important features of their lives, due to experience machines or malicious fake-friends, or from the lives of those who spend all their hours on the couch playing video games and eating pizza.

In subsequent chapters we will discuss views that attribute intrinsic value to things other than pleasures and pains. In each case, when something other than pleasure is proposed as being intrinsically good for us, the hedonist will ask: what if you had that thing but got no pleasure from it? What if you had lots of friends, achieved lots of things, and got everything you wanted, but none of it was enjoyable? Would this be a good life? The hedonist says it wouldn't be.

2.6 Life Satisfaction

There is another view about well-being that is very much like hedonism: the **life satisfaction view**. According to this view, how well-off I am at any given time is determined by my degree of satisfaction at that time about my whole life (Sumner 1996: 172). If I am satisfied with my whole life, then I am well-off; if not, I am not. The more satisfied I am, the better-off I am. According to Wayne Sumner, being satisfied with your life involves two components: an *experiential* component, which involves feeling fulfilled with your life, and a *cognitive* component, or a judgment that life is going well according to your own standards (1996: 172). This view is sufficiently similar to hedonism that it faces many of the same challenges. For example, if you were in an experience machine, you might have feelings of fulfillment and judge that your life is living up to your standards, only because you don't know you are in the machine.

Sumner adds a further element to the life satisfaction view: one is well-off only if one is *authentically* happy. You are not authentically happy if, for example, your life is not in fact meeting up to the standards that you judge it is. (In the experience machine, for example, your life would likely not really be meeting the standards you have set for a good life for yourself.) Thus Sumner's life satisfaction view is a kind of hybrid version of hedonism, much like Feldman's truth-adjusted hedonism.

There are differences between the views, however, due to the fact that life satisfaction views, unlike hedonistic views, focus on *one particular sort* of satisfaction. We might wonder: why think that the degree of satisfaction about one's whole life is the *only* sort of satisfaction that matters? If we think it is good to be satisfied with one's whole life, why not think it is also good to be satisfied with other things, like how one's children are faring? The life satisfactionist's thought might be that your attitude towards your whole life will take into account such things as how your children are faring, or anything else you think is important. Still, we might wonder: what if you are not good at thinking about your whole life? That is, what if, when thinking about your whole life, you tend to ignore some parts of it that really are important to your well-being? Furthermore: suppose at some time I am not having any particular attitudes at all concerning my whole life. I am neither satisfied nor dissatisfied, because I just don't have any opinion at all about my whole life.

My attitudes are directed at smaller things, like my current sensations. How well-off am I at such times? It seems that the life satisfaction view entails that I have no well-being level at all at those times. The life satisfaction theorist might say that what is important is not your *actual* level of satisfaction with your whole life, but the level of satisfaction you *would* have if you were to consider your whole life, whether you actually consider it or not. According to Tatarkiewicz, "Potential, not actual, satisfaction is all that is required for happiness" (1976: 10). But this move raises other problems. If you are not actually experiencing any enjoyment, how can you be well-off merely because you *would* experience enjoyment if you contemplated your life? And *how well* are things going for you in light of this merely counterfactual enjoyment? Furthermore, we might wonder about the implications of this view for someone who was cognitively incapable of grasping the notion of their life as a whole. Such a person might well be dissatisfied with their whole life if they were able to contemplate it – but that is only because if they were able to contemplate it, *they would be a much different person* than the person they actually are in virtue of their enhanced cognitive capacities.

Hedonism and the life satisfaction view have another important thing in common: they are the views that are most commonly presupposed by social science research into well-being. We will discuss this research in chapter 6.

2.7   Further Reading

Classic statements and defenses of hedonism can be found in Epicurus's *Letter to Menoeceus* and *Principal Doctrines* (1964), Jeremy Bentham's *Principles of Morals and Legislation* (1962 [1789]), J.S. Mill's *Utilitarianism* (1861) and Henry Sidgwick's *The Methods of Ethics* (1907, esp. pp. 396–7). In the last decade hedonism has found several defenders, including Fred Feldman (2004), Roger Crisp (2006) and your humble author (2009). Feldman defends hedonism by offering several varieties of the view to suit different intuitions; some of them might be considered "hybrid" versions of hedonism. For interesting recent work on the nature of pleasure, see Feldman (2004), who defends the attitudinal view of pleasure; Chris Heathwood (2007), who explains pleasure in terms of desire; and Roger Crisp (2006, ch. 4) and Aaron Smuts (2011), who defend a distinctive feeling view of pleasure. Wayne Sumner (1996) and Valerie Tiberius (2006) defend life satisfaction accounts of happiness. See ch. 5 of Feldman (2010) for extended critical discussion of such theories. Critiques of hedonism are abundant; see, for example, Chapter X, section iii of Aristotle's *Nicomachean Ethics* (1976); Franz Brentano's *Origin of Our Knowledge of Right and Wrong* (1902 [1889], pp. 87–8); Brentano's *The Foundation and Construction of Ethics* (Brentano 2009 [1952], p. 164), Richard Kraut's *What Is Good and Why* (Kraut 2007: 120–30), and Thomas Carson's *Value and the Good Life* (Carson 2000: 2). There is plenty of literature on Nozick's experience machine argument; see, for example, Jason Kawall's defense of mental state theories (Kawall 1999).

3
Desires

While we think of pleasure as an important part of a good life, perhaps there is a further explanation for this fact: pleasure is something that we all *desire* (and pain is something we all want to avoid). According to the **desire fulfillment view**, what makes life go well, most fundamentally, is getting what we want, and what makes life go badly is failing to get what we want. So a life full of pleasure is likely to be a life in which the individual is getting what she wants. But we might want other things too, so other sorts of lives could also be good for someone; and if someone happens not to want pleasure, the pleasant life wouldn't be good for that person. In order to understand the desire fulfillment view, we should first figure out what we are talking about when we talk about desire.

3.1 What Desires Are

Recall that in our discussion of pleasure, we made a distinction between feelings and attitudes. Desire is an attitude we can take towards things; desires have objects. It is not a feeling. Sometimes when we desire something, there are feelings we are having. For example, suppose I see a bag of potato chips. I have an urge to eat the potato chips. I feel grumbling in my stomach. The grumbling feeling is not the same thing as the desire to eat. The grumbling feeling causes me to have a desire to eat the chips. But the grumbling is just a feeling; it does not have an object; it is not *about* the chips or anything else.

A desire can be fulfilled or frustrated. It is fulfilled when the desirer gets the thing desired; it is frustrated when the desirer does not get the thing desired. A desire may be fulfilled or frustrated even if the desirer does not realize this. If I desire that the Yankees win the World Series, but I am stranded in Antarctica during October and have no way to know who wins, and they do win while I am away, my desire is fulfilled despite the fact I do not realize it. To say that a desire is fulfilled is *not* to say that the desirer has a feeling of fulfillment or satisfaction, and to say that a desire is frustrated is *not* to say that the desirer has a feeling of frustration. This is very important – if it were feelings of satisfaction that mattered, there would be little difference between the desire fulfillment view and hedonism. If you think a feeling of fulfillment is what is important, you are probably a hedonist, not a desire fulfillment theorist.

Like pleasures, desires come in different intensities; there are strong desires and weak desires. If I haven't eaten food in several hours, I will have a strong desire to eat food. If I am not hungry, but see a delicious-looking cake, I will have a relatively weak desire to eat the cake. Also like pleasures, desires come in durations. We have all sorts of desires that are mere whims, fleeting and quickly forgotten; but we have other desires that persist, such as desires to achieve career goals.

Some things we desire for themselves; we desire them not because we desire something else, but intrinsically. Other things we desire merely extrinsically. For example, when I desire to eat cake, it is not the eating of the cake that I desire for itself. I desire to eat the cake because I expect to enjoy it. If I didn't expect that, I wouldn't desire to eat the cake. So my desire to eat the cake is merely extrinsic. But my desire for the enjoyable taste experience is intrinsic. I don't desire that experience because of some other thing I desire; I desire it for itself. It is common to say that it is only intrinsic desires that matter to well-being; let us agree to this restriction (Brandt 1979: 111; Heathwood 2005: 489). Suppose I am leaving the house and notice that the sky is cloudy; I then form a desire to bring an umbrella with me in order to stay dry. But then I am distracted by a squirrel, and forget to bring the umbrella. As it turns out, it doesn't rain, and I stay dry. My extrinsic desire to bring an umbrella was frustrated. Am I worse off because this desire was frustrated? It does not seem so. I only had that desire because I wanted to stay dry, and I did stay dry anyway. This seems to support the thought that only intrinsic desires matter to well-being. From now on "desire" will mean "intrinsic desire" unless noted otherwise.

3.2 The Desire Fulfillment View

Given these assumptions about desire, we may formulate the desire fulfillment view as follows. What is intrinsically good for an individual is the fulfillment of a desire; what is intrinsically bad for an individual is the frustration of a desire. How good or bad it is for someone to have a desire fulfilled depends on how long the desire lasts and how intense it is; the more intense and long-lasting the desire is, the better it is for it to be fulfilled, and the worse it is for it to be frustrated. To determine the value of an individual's life, simply add the values of the desire fulfillments and frustrations it contains. Thus, a life containing many long-lasting, intense desires that are fulfilled, and not many frustrations, is a good life for the person living it.

If you want the number of stars in the universe to be even, and it is even, you get what you want – but you didn't do anything to make it so. We might think that merely getting what you want is not the only thing that matters; it is also important to make some effort to get it. Call this the **achievement view** (Keller 2004). According to the achievement view, we look not only at how long-lasting and intense a desire is, but the extent of the effort exerted to see it fulfilled. The more effort you put into achieving some goal, the better it is for you that the goal is reached, and the worse it is for you that it is not reached. I'll focus on the simpler desire fulfillment view, since the problems for that view tend to be faced also by the Achievement View.

Why should we think that desire is particularly relevant to well-being? The most important reason is the thought that well-being is something that *resonates* with us (Railton 2003: 47; Dorsey 2012: 275). The best life for a person should be a life that the person cares about. Suppose Marie is a talented pianist, but does not want to play the piano. She pursues the life of a pianist out of a sense of obligation to her parents, who invested a great deal of money in her training. Her deepest desire is to be a scientist, and she would be content never to play the piano again. Marie's life probably strikes you as not the best life for her. Perhaps it is good for her parents that she pursues the life of a pianist, but it is not good for her. The desire fulfillment view explains why her life is not so great: her most intense, longest-lasting desire is frustrated.

Marie's story leads us to note a possible source of confusion about the notion of desire. In one sense, it is natural to say that Marie is not doing what she most desires. But someone might counter, "obviously what she most desires is to please her parents! Otherwise she would not be playing the piano. So she is, in fact, doing what she most desires to do." On this way of thinking about desire, any time we voluntarily do something, it must be because of some sufficiently strong desire we have. There are at least two distinctions we might draw that can help us see why we think that, in one sense, Marie does what she most desires, but in another sense, she doesn't. (i) David Lewis distinguishes "warm" and "cold" desires (Lewis 1988). For Marie, the desire to be a scientist is "warm." When she thinks of being a scientist, she gets excited; she is pleased at the prospect of becoming a scientist. Not so with playing the piano. Though in some sense she desires to do it, because she cares about what her parents think of her choices, playing the piano does not excite her. Perhaps the desire fulfillment view would be more plausible if the desires it takes to be good to fulfill are only the warm desires, the ones that resonate with us. (Note that to say a desire is warm is not to say that the person gets feelings of satisfaction when it is fulfilled; a warm desire can be fulfilled even if the desirer doesn't know it is fulfilled. It is the *prospect* of its fulfillment that excites the desirer.) (ii) Thomas Nagel distinguishes "motivated" and "unmotivated" desires (Nagel 1986: 151). Motivated desires are desires that we have only because we "recognize that there is reason to do or want something" (p. 151). Marie's desire to play the piano is motivated; she has this desire only because she takes her parents' preferences as providing a reason to play the piano. Her desire to be a scientist is not motivated; she just wants to be one. Perhaps the desire fulfillment view would be more plausible if the desires it takes to be good to fulfill are only the unmotivated desires.

Like hedonism, the desire fulfillment view is not elitist. It does not matter what you desire; as long as you get it, things are going well for you to that extent. It is possible to make mistakes in what you desire, but only insofar as desiring some things will make it more difficult to get other things you want more. So if you really want to smoke methamphetamines, and you do it, you get something you want, which is good for you; but if this causes you to lose your job and your teeth, you will fail to get other things you want more, which is bad for you. Desiring the crystal meth is a mistake for that reason. Besides that sort of mistake, it does not matter what sorts of things you desire. In fact, if you desire to be in pain, the desire fulfillment view entails that being in pain is good for you, contrary to what hedonism says. The desire fulfillment view does not dictate what you ought to want.

Some may be attracted to desire-based views of well-being due to deep philosophical considerations about the nature of the universe. Many philosophers are attracted to a naturalistic view of reality. It is not easy to say what naturalism amounts to, but we may think of it as the view that the only things that exist are, or are composed of, the things (objects, properties, relations) that are studied by the sciences: physics, chemistry, biology, geology, psychology, etc. These would include atoms, the parts of atoms, forces, fields, charges, molecules, planets, plants, animals, rocks, desires, and pleasures, as well as things that are composed out of such things, such as tables and computers. Suppose we think those sorts of things are the only things that there are. We might wonder: where do values fit in? Could there really be such a thing as the property *being good for people*? And yet it really does seem like some things are good for us and other things are bad for us. Why does it seem this way? The desire theorist has a plausible explanation for this appearance: we are led to think that some things are good for us and other things are bad for us because we desire some things and are averse to others. For something to be good for me, then, is just for me to desire it. Goodness gets reduced to desire. Since desire, as a subject of study of psychology, is a naturalistically respectable property, we can be naturalists and still believe that there are things that are good for us.

The desire fulfillment view also seems better equipped than hedonism to account for the value of life in an experience machine. Someone living such a life would think she was getting everything she wanted in life, but in fact would not be. Remember that to have a desire fulfilled is not to have a feeling of fulfillment or satisfaction; it is just for the object of the desire to obtain. So although she might think her life is going terrifically well, because she desires to be rich and powerful or to be achieving great things and she believes she is getting those things, she in fact is not getting them, because she is in a machine. Therefore she is just wrong to think her life is going well. And that is what many people think is the correct thing to say about such a life.

3.3 Defective Desires

The non-elitism of the desire fulfillment view is supposed to be a good feature of the view, but the view might actually be *too* non-elitist. There are some things that resonate with people even though they probably shouldn't resonate. Since there are no restrictions on what sorts of desires matter to well-being, we can imagine someone with immoral, base, or trivial desires who gets everything he wants, and therefore lives a wonderful life according to the desire fulfillment view, but who does not seem really to be living such a great life. An example of someone with *immoral desires* would be the person who desires to torture animals. An example of someone with *trivial desires* would be the person who desires to count the leaves on every tree in his yard. An example of someone with **base desires** would be the person who desires nothing more than to play video games and eat pizza. Assuming that fulfilling these desires does not lead you to have other important desires that go unfulfilled, the desire fulfillment view would count a life full of these sorts of fulfilled desires as one of the best lives you could live. You might find this doubtful. On the other hand, the desire fulfillment view can be defended in the same way hedonists defend their view against such arguments. We might say that although these sorts of lives are bad in a way – they are immoral, or pointless – they are not bad with respect to *well-being*.

Another difficult problem for the desire fulfillment view involves what have been referred to as *adaptive preferences*. Sometimes the world seems to shape our desires in problematic ways. In some societies women are severely oppressed, and are not allowed to work outside the home, drive a car, or receive an education. Sometimes, despite such restrictions, individuals may be perfectly content. They might lose the desire to do any of those things, retaining only desires that they can realistically fulfill (Sen 1999: 20). Sometimes they even believe it would be wrong for a woman to do those things (Nussbaum 2011: 83–4). The Desire Fulfillment View sees no problem here; everyone is getting what they want, so everyone is well-off. But there does seem to be a problem. The oppressive social structure is deforming people's desires. Looking only at the extent to which such desires are satisfied seems unlikely to tell us how well-off someone really is.

There are also desires that are based on faulty information. If I am thirsty and desire to drink what is in the glass on the table, thinking it is just plain water, I may get what I want; but if it is poisoned water, it does not seem like it is good for me to drink the water. But perhaps this is not a problem. After all, drinking poison will cause me to have other unfulfilled desires, which would be bad for me. So the desire fulfillment view does not seem threatened by this case.

Consider also the desire to have a bad life. When someone has such a desire, paradox can result, if the desire fulfillment view is true. Suppose the person has only that one desire, the desire to have a bad life. Now suppose the desire is fulfilled, because the person is having a bad life. Since it is good to fulfill a desire, the person is having a good life, contrary to our supposition. But supposing the person is having a good life, the desire is frustrated, and so since it is bad to have a desire frustrated, the person is having a bad life. Thus if this person is having a good life, he is having a bad life, and if he is having a bad life, he is having a good life. That is a paradox! Of course, nobody in fact has only one desire. But the paradox can arise in other cases too. Just imagine that someone has some desires frustrated and the same number of desires fulfilled. Now imagine the person desires to have a bad life. The same paradox will arise (Heathwood 2005; Bradley 2009: ch. 1).

3.4 Sophisticated Desire Views

In response to problems involving defective desires, the desire theorist might move to a more sophisticated view according to which some desires – the crazy, or immoral, or inauthentic, or uninformed ones – are not good for us to satisfy. And in fact this is the move that is made by the vast majority of desire theorists, including Sidgwick (1907) and Richard Brandt (1979). But how do we rule out such desires without violating the spirit of the desire fulfillment view? Remember that the main attraction of the view is the thought that well-being should *resonate* with us; we should be excited by it, drawn to it, and find it desirable. If something does resonate, why would we want to say it is not good for us?

According to one more sophisticated version of the desire fulfillment view, to figure out what is good for a person, we do not look at what the person actually desires. Rather, we look at what the person would desire if she were fully informed about all her possible future life plans. We are to imagine that the person would be vividly aware of what each life would be like (Sidgwick 1907: 111–12; Brandt 1979: ch. VI). Consider, for example, the person whose desires have been warped by oppression so that she does not desire to get an education or drive a car. The thought is that such a person, if fully aware of what a more free life would be like, would prefer such a life over her actual life. Or perhaps she wouldn't, but if she really did continue to prefer the less free life after fully and vividly imagining what freedom would involve, it is plausible to think that the less free life really would be better for her. Similarly for the leaf counter, kitten torturer, and pizza eater.

But the question is, why should we assume such people would change their desires given the knowledge of what alternative lives would be like? We are not supposed to imagine that any lives are *objectively* better for us than others, so why think that one would be chosen over the other given full information? Furthermore, even if we suppose that someone would change her desires under such circumstances, why think the counterfactual desires are the ones to look at? If I do not want to live a certain sort of life, even if I *would* like that life under *other* circumstances, it violates the resonance constraint to say that such a life is *actually* good for me.

The desire theorist could give a more modest role to a resonance constraint. Suppose there are certain things that we think are good to desire, and other things that are bad to desire. Maybe listening to Beethoven is something that is good to desire, and being in pain is bad to desire. We might be willing to say that there is an objective fact of the matter that these things are good or bad to desire. But we might also say that it is not good to get the things that are good to desire unless we desire them (Kraut 1994: 43–5). So, although listening to Beethoven would be good for me if I were to desire to listen to Beethoven, it fails to be good for me if I don't desire it. On the other hand, even if I desire to be in pain, it would not be good for me to be in pain. So nothing is in fact good for me unless I desire it; but there are things that, objectively, I ought to desire. Of course, this view requires us to say something about what makes something good to desire. If we are concerned about naturalism, we might wonder how it is possible for something to be, objectively, something that is good to desire.

The three main options for the desire fulfillment view so far, then, are: (1) a simple view that counts all desire fulfillments towards well-being, no matter how bizarre, trivial, warped, or immoral; (2) an "idealized" desire view that identifies what is good for us with what we *would* desire under certain ideal conditions, such as the possession of full information about alternatives; (3) a "hybrid" view that identifies certain things as objectively worthy of desire, and says that it is good for us to desire and obtain those things.

3.5 Past Desires, Unknown Fulfillments, and Posthumous Harms

Many of our desires change over time. Some of these changes are not very interesting. At noon I get hungry and desire to eat food; then I eat some food and am no longer hungry, so I lose the desire to eat. There is nothing interesting about this. But other changes are more interesting. Suppose Jerry is an art student who desires to become a professional artist. He invests a lot of time and effort into attempting to become an artist. Later on, his desire fades; he no longer wishes to be an artist. Now he prefers to be an auto mechanic. Would it be intrinsically good for him to become an artist once his desire to become an artist has faded? It would not seem so. Yet according to the simple version of the desire fulfillment view, it would be good for him. After all, he had a strong and long-lasting desire to be an artist, so becoming an artist would satisfy a very important desire he had. This would constitute an important welfare improvement in his life, according to the desire fulfillment view.

Perhaps, instead, the desire fulfillment theorist should say that what is good for us is to get what we want, *while we want it* (Heathwood 2005). Getting something we used to want but don't want anymore is not good for us.

But this might be too hasty. Other examples might pull us in the opposite direction. Suppose Jerry does become an artist, and desires very strongly to have his work displayed in the Museum of Modern Art. But just before his work can be displayed there, he dies. Some would say that, for Jerry's sake, it would be good for the museum to display his work even though he is dead. We might lend further support to this notion by remembering that according to the desire fulfillment theorist, you need not be aware that your desire is satisfied in order for it to be satisfied, and that it is good to have a desire satisfied even if you are not aware of it. So being dead should be no obstacle to being benefited by having your desires satisfied. We might imagine that at the time of his death, Jerry is on a trip in the wilderness and is trampled by a wildebeest. He never knows whether his work has been displayed. Would it matter whether his work was displayed the day before his death or the day after? We might think that could not possibly matter, and so if we think it is good for him to display his work the day before his death, it must also be good for him to display it the day after.

And yet, it seems there must be limits to posthumous benefits and harms of this sort. When deciding how to resolve land disputes in the Middle East, should those living today take into account the desires of those who lived in biblical times? Decisions made by people now will determine whether the desires had by those who have been dead for thousands of years are fulfilled or frustrated. But it is hard to believe that we can benefit or harm those long-dead people. So there is a real challenge for the desire fulfillment theorist here.

How we deal with the issue of past desires and changing desires is of pressing importance in, for example, cases of advance directives. Often people express desires concerning what medical treatment will be given to them should something happen to them – for example, they might say that they do not want certain treatments should they get Alzheimer's or suffer a debilitating injury. Continued life under such circumstances strikes some people as undesirable. But of course, at a later time, their opinion about continued life might change, since people are not always good at figuring out what they would want if they were to become severely disabled. How, then, should we treat advance directives? Should we look at the past desire or the present desire? And if we can't determine what someone's present desire is (because they are unable to communicate, for example), should we assume that their past desire is a good guide to what their present desire is?

These issues involving past desires raise a further question: when a past desire is fulfilled, *when* is the desirer benefited? Is it at the time the desire is fulfilled, or at the time the individual had the desire? If the former, then in the case of posthumous harm and benefit, we would have to say that someone can be well-off or badly off at a time after they die. If the latter, we are committed to saying that events that happen in the future can affect how well-off someone is right now. Both of these results seem surprising.

Derek Parfit presented a problem for desire fulfillment views that is related to the problems just discussed (Parfit 1984: 494). You meet a stranger who has a life-threatening illness. You come to have a desire that this stranger be cured of his illness. You go your separate ways and never see the stranger again; you never find out what happened to him. Suppose the stranger in fact gets cured. Does this make your life go better for you, even though you never know about it? This seems hard to believe.

In response, the desire fulfillment theorist might say that the desires relevant to your well-being are desires that are *about you* (Overvold 1984: 499). Desires about others do not affect your well-being. Thus it does not benefit you if the stranger is cured, even though you want him to be. But what about those who are close to us, our children, friends and other loved ones? Why wouldn't it be good for us to have desires about those people satisfied? These are desires that are very important to us.[3]

Another possible move is to say that in order for a desire fulfillment to make your life go better, you also must *believe* your desire has been fulfilled. In Parfit's example, you fail to have any such belief, so even if the stranger was cured, you are not benefited. This move would also have implications for posthumous benefit and harm. If someone is dead, he can no longer come to believe that his desire is satisfied. So it may be impossible to harm or benefit someone posthumously given the belief requirement. But this will depend on how we deal with time. When must you believe that your desire is satisfied? At the time it is satisfied, or before or after? If Jerry believes before he dies that his work will be displayed, and it is displayed after he dies, has the belief condition been met? This would have strange implications too. Imagine that Mary also wanted her work displayed, but did not believe it would be. And suppose we must decide whether to display Jerry or Mary's work; only one artist can be chosen. In making our decision about which artist to display, in trying to produce the most benefit, should we first ask which of them believed their work would be displayed? That may seem implausible.

---

[3] Overvold (1984) argues that this move is required in order to make the desire fulfillment view compatible with self-sacrifice.

It might seem equally implausible even if the case involves current beliefs. Suppose Jerry and Mary aren't dead, just on safari in some remote location never to return; suppose Jerry believes his work is being displayed, and Mary does not, but both want their work displayed. Do we benefit Jerry by displaying his work but not Mary by displaying hers? This seems equally implausible. Maybe the belief requirement is not such a good idea after all.

To take stock, we now have even more options for the desire fulfillment theory. In addition to the simple theory, the idealized desire theory, and the hybrid theory, we now also have (4) a version that assigns value only to desires about the agent, and (5) a version that assigns value to satisfied desires only when the agent believes they are satisfied. And for each of these versions we also have another version that ascribes value to *successful effort or achievement* rather than mere desire. Like hedonism, the desire fulfillment theory is flexible. It is not easy to find an argument against desire fulfillment views that applies to all versions of the view. Thus, when evaluating the desire fulfillment theory, it is important to be clear about which version of the view we are evaluating.

3.6 Further Reading

Henry Sidgwick set the stage for contemporary discussions of desire fulfillment theories in Chapter IX of *The Methods of Ethics* (1907). Richard Brandt gives an important account of what makes a desire rational in Part I of *A Theory of the Good and the Right* (1979). Well-known critiques of various sorts of desire-based theories can be found in Derek Parfit (1984, Appendix I), Richard Kraut (1994), David Sobel (1994), Connie Rosati (1995), and Robert Adams (1999: 84–93). Chris Heathwood (2005) has recently provided a clear defense of desire fulfillment views against some of these objections. The value of achievement has recently been defended by Simon Keller (2004) and Gwen Bradford (2013). For discussion of the problem of adaptive preferences, see Amartya Sen (1999), Martha Nussbaum (2011), Jennifer Hawkins (2006), and Serene Khader (2011).

4
Capabilities and Human Nature

When we reflect on examples like the kitten torturer, the experience machine, the leaf counter, and the oppressed person whose preferences have adapted to her oppression, we may begin to think that a life can be lacking in well-being even though the person living the life doesn't believe anything is lacking and is perfectly content with her life. One natural thought is that these lives are missing some crucial part of what it is to be human. **Perfectionism** is the view that what is best for a human is to develop those capacities that constitute human nature, such as rational and physical capacities. Developing those capacities involves such things as acquiring knowledge, honing one's talents, and being healthy. Doing these things promotes well-being even if the person developing them does not care about doing them.

4.1 Perfectionism

There is a wide variety of views that might be characterized as "perfectionist." I will begin by characterizing perfectionism at a very abstract level, and then look at some more concrete versions of the view.

One important feature of most perfectionist views is that they characterize what is good for an individual by appeal to *what kind of individual it is*. As Philippa Foot says, "To flourish is here to instantiate the life form of that species, and to know whether an individual is or is not as it should be, one must know the life form of the species" (Foot 2001: 91). The specific features of a good life for a human are different from the specific features of a good life for a dog. At a more abstract level, what is good for a human and what is good for a dog can be seen as the same: an individual is best off when it exemplifies, to the greatest degree, certain features that are, in some way (to be discussed below), tied to the kind or species of thing it is. Compare this to what a hedonist says. According to hedonism, the best life for a human and the best life for a dog are the same: they contain lots of pleasure and little pain. Since humans and dogs are different in certain important respects, the perfectionist will say that the best life for a human might contain features that are not part of the best life for a dog. This is an important selling point for perfectionism. It allows the perfectionist to deny that a life full of eating things, chasing cats, wrestling with other dogs, and barking, but devoid of any other intellectual or physical achievements, is the best life for a human, even if the human somehow gets lots of pleasure out of those activities. But it does seem as if such a life would be good for a dog. Call this feature of perfectionism *species-relativity*.

Perfectionists deny that what is good for you depends on what you think about the matter. It is not up to you what kind of thing you are; so it is not up to you what is good for you. Thus perfectionists think that well-being is *objective*. If you are not interested in developing the features that make you human, then unfortunately for you, you are not interested in your own well-being. You are making an important mistake.

What is intrinsically good for us is developing our human capacities. But what is intrinsically bad for us? This seems harder to say. We might say that it is intrinsically bad to fail to develop our human capacities. But we all fail, to some extent, to develop those capacities. When this happens, there is an absence of what would be good for us; but the mere absence of what is good is not *intrinsically* bad. It might be best to say that there is some threshold of development such that if you fail to develop your capacities to that threshold, things are going badly for you. What is bad for you is a deficiency in your capabilities. You do not have a deficiency merely in virtue of failing to develop your capacities to the greatest possible extent; you have a deficiency if your development does not meet the threshold.

Perfectionism, like the other views discussed so far, is a *monistic* view, according to which all intrinsic goods are fundamentally similar. While different sorts of thing might be the objects of desire, if desire satisfactionism were true, the intrinsic goods would have in common that they were desired; while human perfection might consist of very different sorts of excellence, if perfectionism were true, those excellences would have in common that they were excellences of human nature.

So perfectionism is an objective, species-relative, monistic theory. It is hard to evaluate Perfectionism until we have more details. Let us next examine what might be meant by "human nature."

4.2 Human Nature, Function, and Distinctiveness

On one way of thinking about human nature, to figure out what human nature is we must figure out what the *function* or *purpose* of a human being is. We are accustomed to thinking about functions and purposes when it comes to artifacts and tools. We know what a hammer is for: it is for pounding in nails. We know that is what it is for, because we invented hammers to do that. A hammer that is hammer-shaped but made of Jell-O is not a good hammer, because it won't do what a hammer is supposed to do. But a human being is not a tool. So how are we to think about the function of a human?

On some religious views, humans *are* a bit like hammers. We were created by a superior being to fulfill some purpose. When we fulfill that purpose, we are doing what we are supposed to do, and are better-off in virtue of this fact. But many of us do not believe in a superior being that created humans.

So the appeal of this sort of view is limited. And in any case, we might wonder: why should I be better-off merely in virtue of fulfilling *someone else's* purposes, even if that someone else is a superior being?

The notion of function need not require a designer. Biological explanations sometimes appeal to the functions of things. We can talk about the function of the human heart – to pump blood – even though nobody invented the heart. But it is less obvious what the function of a whole person is. When talking about the function of the human heart, we look to the larger thing of which it is a part: the human body. The heart fulfills its function when it serves a certain role in keeping the human body functioning. To figure out the function of a human being, perhaps we need to look to some larger thing of which it is a part. A natural thing to look at is the *species*. This might lead us to say that, just as the function of the heart is to help the body survive, the function of a human being is to promote the survival of the species *homo sapiens*. Unfortunately, if this is the function of a human being, it seems unlikely that individual human well-being can be understood in terms of fulfilling the function of a human being. Sometimes doing what is best for the species might be bad for me as an individual. For example, if I needed to sacrifice my health or my life for the lives of several other humans, it seems wrong to say that this sacrifice is good for me, even if it would help preserve humanity.

Sometimes when we think about something's function, we seem to have in mind something that is *distinctive* about that thing – something that sets it apart from other things. For instance, here is Aristotle:

> But presumably to say that happiness is the supreme good seems a platitude, and some more distinctive account of it is still required. This might perhaps be achieved by grasping what is the function of man...What, then, can this possibly be? Clearly life is a thing shared also by plants, and we are looking for man's proper function; so we must exclude from our definition the life that consists in nutrition and growth. Next in order would be a sort of sentient life; but this too we see is shared by horses and cattle and animals of all kinds. There remains, then, a practical life of the rational part. (Aristotle, *Nicomachean Ethics*, 1976, I.vii, 1097b22–1098a8)

Aristotle is looking for what sets humans apart from plants and other animals. Perhaps this is an unusual way of thinking about "function" – but it seems like it might be a promising way to locate which features of a person are of particular importance in determining well-being, since we are looking for an explanation of why a life of mere pleasure might be less than optimal for a person. Merely being alive and having feelings (such as feelings of pleasure) does not distinguish us as human. Rather, it is our rationality. There are different ways we might understand what rationality amounts to, but let us suppose that to be rational is to be responsive to reasons: to be able to contemplate reasons for or against doing or believing something and for one's behavior and beliefs to be guided by the grasping of such reasons.

Unfortunately, no matter how we understand rationality, there seems to be no guarantee that human beings are the *only* beings that are rational. And in any case, it is unclear why distinctiveness should be so crucial. Suppose we were to discover that dolphins are rational in ways very much like the ways humans are rational. Should this lead us to revise what we think about *human* well-being? It is hard to see why it should have any relevance.

4.3   The Essence of Humanity

When we ask what it is to be a human, we might be asking about the *essence* of humanity. The *essential features* of a species are the features such that nothing could be a member of that species unless it had those features. What are the essential features of a human being? And how do we figure this out?

To tell whether some feature of humans is essential or merely accidental, we can start by looking to see whether any humans lack that feature. For instance, we can tell that having brown hair is not essential to humans because there are many humans who lack brown hair. But sometimes things are not so easy. There might be a feature possessed by all humans merely accidentally. For instance, all humans live on Earth.

But this need not be so; if humans established a colony on Mars, they would not cease to be humans. To tell whether some feature possessed by all humans is essential, we have to rely on our imaginations. We would have to try to imagine some creatures lacking that feature and ask whether such creatures would be humans or not. Sometimes it is argued that, in addition to possibly being distinctive of us, *rationality* is essential to humans. If we imagined some creatures who lacked rationality, then no matter how much they looked like us, they would not be humans, it might be said. Life and sentience are also candidates; perhaps beings that were not living and could not have sensations or consciousness could not possibly be humans. Perhaps we are also essentially physical beings – beings that take up space and are made of physical stuff. How could an individual not take up any space and still be a human being?

It seems that it is at least as plausible that we are essentially physical beings as it is that we are essentially rational. This is problematic if we then want to appeal to essential features in order to assess well-being. If humans essentially take up space, are we better-off when we take up more space? Are the largest people the best off? It does not seem that what is essential to us is what makes us *what we are*, in any sense that could be relevant to well-being.

Thomas Hurka has suggested that essence and distinctiveness can be combined to yield a more plausible perfectionist view. According to Hurka's perfectionism, what is valuable is the development of those properties that are essential to human beings "qua living things," or properties that are both essential to humans and distinctive of living things (Hurka 1993: 16). According to Hurka, this version of perfectionism entails that what is good for us is to develop our physical nature, our theoretical rationality, and our practical rationality (Hurka 1993: 37). Thus, in order to have the best life for a human, one would need to be physically fit and healthy, acquire a lot of knowledge (especially knowledge of very general, deep facts about the nature of the universe), and be morally and prudentially virtuous. These do seem to be things we value in life. They are also things that are absent from some of the problematic lives we have discussed. Someone in an experience machine lacks important knowledge about the universe, and is not developing her physical capacities, among other things.

We might wonder, though, whether Hurka's perfectionism captures all there is to well-being. For example, you can be healthy and rational without enjoying yourself. But a life with no enjoyment does not seem like the best sort of life. Of course, there are different reasons one might have no enjoyment. If you are depressed, you might be unable to enjoy things that other people would enjoy. Depression is a kind of mental illness, and so if you are depressed you are not perfectly healthy in all respects. So the perfectionist can explain why your life is not going well if you are not enjoying yourself because you are depressed. But you might be failing to enjoy yourself while at the same time being healthy, rational, and knowledgeable.

A deeper problem for Hurka's view is that it seems to rely on an implausible view about what is essential to humanity. There are members of *homo sapiens* that do not have the properties identified by Hurka as essential to humanity: those with serious brain damage, and very young infants, for example, do not have the sort of rationality that is alleged by Hurka to be part of the human essence, but they are human beings nonetheless. Since any very sophisticated sort of rationality is unlikely to be part of the human essence, it seems unlikely that restricting our focus to essential features of humanity is going to yield anything of interest when it comes to human well-being.

4.4   The Character of Humanity

Perhaps a more promising strategy than focusing on what is essential to humanity would be to focus on what is *characteristic* of humans (Foot 2001: ch. 2; Hursthouse 1999: ch. 9). Rationality might be characteristic of humanity even if many humans are not rational. It may help to consider some things we say about other species. For example, here is a statement from Hursthouse: "Wolves hunt in packs; a 'free-rider' wolf that doesn't join in the hunt fails to act well and is thereby defective" (1999: 201). Here are some things we say about other species: "Horses are quadrupeds." "Mosquitoes carry malaria." "Mosquitoes are widespread." These statements all seem true. But a horse can lose a leg and still be a horse. So "horses are quadrupeds" does not mean "necessarily, all horses have four legs." It is a statement about the kind *horse*.[4] Similarly for "wolves hunt in packs." "Mosquitoes carry malaria" is true even though *most* mosquitoes do *not* carry malaria. So statements about kinds can be true even when most members of the kind do not have the feature in question. "Mosquitoes are widespread" is true even though *no individual mosquito* is widespread – being widespread is not something a single mosquito can possibly be! So statements about kinds can be true even when no members of the kind have the feature in question (for a good recent discussion of generics, see Liebesman 2011).

The proposal, then, is that some feature F is part of human nature just in case humans are F – that is, the kind *human* has F. What features does the kind *human* have? It will be very difficult to say in general what must be the case in order for the kind *human* to have some feature; as we've seen, it need not be the case that all or most humans have that feature (Liebesman 2011). Let us first attempt to rely on our intuitive judgments on the matter. It does seem correct to say that humans are rational, intelligent, creative, and athletic. So a human who exemplified these features to a high degree would be doing well on perfectionist grounds. Unfortunately, when we remove our rose-colored glasses, it also seems right to say that humans are cruel, selfish, and dishonest. So a human who exemplified these features would also be doing well. This is an unwelcome result.

Rather than relying on our intuitive judgments, we might look to biology and see what features a biologist would say are characteristic of *Homo sapiens*. Here is the definition of *Homo sapiens* on the website *Biology Online*:

---

[4] Hursthouse (1999: 203) says that these evaluations are "judgements about individuals as members of a certain species or subspecies" – but it seems better to say that they are about the species themselves, since species can do things no member of them can do (like be widespread).

The species group of bipedal hominins characterized by having higher and vertical forehead, brain volume of about 1,400 cc, smaller teeth and jaw, and prominent chin relative to earlier hominins. They are also identified as hominins that created and used more complex tools, solved problems through sense and reasoning, used symbols and language, created complex social structures, and showed in due course behavioral modernity following many years of existence.[5]

Some of the features characteristic of humanity, from the standpoint of biology, are features that are utterly irrelevant to well-being, such as the sizes of our foreheads and teeth. Others, such as problem-solving, might be relevant to well-being in some way; but problem-solving can be directed towards problems that are important or trivial, good or evil. Once again, we should not have to keep our rose-colored glasses on when developing a view of human nature for the perfectionist to use.

We might think the *species-relative* aspect of perfectionism is especially problematic in light of the way biologists currently think about species – or rather, the many ways in which they do. Before the development of modern biology, it was common to think that individuals were divided neatly (by God, perhaps) into distinct species, and that species boundaries were necessary and immutable. But now the evidence tells us this is not the case. Species gradually evolve from other species. Often there are grey areas in which it is not clear where species boundaries ought to be drawn. Biologists use a variety of species concepts; some are based on inherent morphological characteristics, others on facts about interbreeding, others on facts about ecological niche. Species membership is, in general, much more fluid and up-for-grabs than we once thought. There are also persuasive arguments that species membership is *not essential* to individuals: that a given individual who is a member of one species might instead have been a member of a different species (LaPorte 1997). Given these facts about species, why think that what species I am a member of makes such a big difference to what is good for me?

[5] http://www.biology-online.org/dictionary/Homo_sapiens, accessed October 21, 2014.

Perfectionists have to delicately thread a needle, including just the right features as part of human nature. They want to include features like rationality, even though such features seem not to be essential to us and need not be distinctive of us. But what reason is there to think that rationality is part of human nature, but other less desirable features, such as cruelty, are not?

4.5 Capabilities and Dignity

Rather than attempt to derive what is good for us from meta-physical facts about essence, Martha Nussbaum argues that what is good for us is tied to the notion of dignity: "some living conditions deliver to people a life that is worthy of the human dignity that they possess, and others do not" (2011: 30). To have a worthwhile human life, to be well-off, is to possess and develop the capabilities required by dignity. While you might have some intuitive notion of what dignity amounts to, Nussbaum admits it is a vague notion. She does not attempt to *derive* what is good for us from an independent notion of dignity, as the perfectionist attempts to derive what is good from an independent notion of human nature. But she does hope that you will agree that certain features of a life are necessary for it to be dignified. She lists ten "Central Capabilities" that she takes to constitute well-being (2011: 33–4):

1. Life (having a life of normal length)
2. Bodily health (including nourishment and shelter)
3. Bodily integrity (freedom from violence)
4. Senses, imagination, and thought (including pleasures)
5. Emotions (attachments and loving relationships)
6. Practical reason (reflecting on one's life plan)
7. Affiliation (forming groups, not being discriminated against)
8. Other species (relationships to nonhumans)
9. Play
10. Control over one's political and material environment

You will probably agree that these capabilities are all good things to have in your life. You might even agree that they are essential to having a good life. But remember that we are attempting to formulate a theory of what is *intrinsically* good for us. You might think that some of these things are merely *instrumentally* good. Is it intrinsically good merely to be able to live a long life? To be able to be healthy? To be able to have a pet dog? To be able to vote and own property? It seems doubtful that this is so. There is more to say about the items on Nussbaum's list; we will discuss some of them in the next chapter.

We might agree with Nussbaum that governments should ensure that individuals have all of these capabilities. And in fact this seems to be what Nussbaum ultimately cares most about. But it does not follow from the fact that governments should ensure that individuals have certain capabilities that these capabilities are intrinsically good for us, rather than very important instrumental goods. One reason to be skeptical that any of the capabilities on Nussbaum's list are intrinsically good for humans is the focus on what we are *able* to do rather than what we *in fact* do. While you might think it is important to have the capabilities Nussbaum lists, it is surely important also to *realize* those capabilities – to actually experience some pleasure, actually associate with other people, actually have a pet dog, rather than merely to have the capability to do these things. How could it be good to have the *capacity* to have something if it weren't good to *actually have* the thing? Surely a life in which one has the capacity to get some pleasure, and actually gets some pleasure, is better than one in which one is capable of doing so but never does. On the other hand, it makes sense for society to ensure that people have the ability to have a dog but much less sense for society to ensure that everyone has a dog whether they want one or not; this lends support to the thought that Nussbaum's list is a list of things society should ensure people have, rather than a list of things that are intrinsically good for people.

A more general worry about Nussbaum's view is that it is unclear whether dignity can play the unifying role she envisions. If we imagine two lives, one of which contains some enjoyments and the other does not, would we say that the life full of enjoyment is more suited to human dignity than the one without? Enjoyment and dignity just seem completely unrelated. If enjoyment enhances the value of your life without enhancing your dignity, then dignity cannot fully explain what makes life go well for you.

4.6 Further Reading

Chapter I of Aristotle's *Nicomachean Ethics* (1976) is the starting place for discussions of perfectionist views. Thomas Hurka's *Perfectionism* (1993) contains a detailed development of perfectionist theories of the good, making use of recent developments in metaphysics and philosophy of language (though Hurka disavows the concept of well-being); also see ch. IV of James Griffin's *Well-Being* (1986). Philippa Foot's *Natural Goodness* (2001) and Richard Kraut's *What is Good and Why* (2007) are prominent recent defenses of an Aristotelian view. For a Nietzschean sort of perfectionism, see ch. 4 of Thomas Carson's *Value and the Good Life* (2000). For recent criticisms of perfectionism, see Philip Kitcher (1999) and Dale Dorsey (2010). Martha Nussbaum and Amartya Sen's "capabilities approach" is broadly perfectionist and has been extremely influential; see Nussbaum's *Creating Capabilities* (2011) for a recent development of that approach.

5
Pluralism

Perhaps the good things in life are not unified by human nature or dignity. A different approach would be just to identify the things we think make our lives better without being concerned about metaphysical questions about essences and natures. **Pluralism** (sometimes called the "objective list" theory) is the view that there are several things that are intrinsically good for us, not unified by anything more than being good for us. A pluralist might identify as intrinsic goods the same list of things that Hurka or Nussbaum would identify; but the pluralist would deny that there is any deeper explanation for why those things are on the list.

Pleasure and desire fulfillment are often listed among the intrinsic goods in life. There are many other candidates, and it would be difficult to discuss them all. Among them are knowledge, virtue, friendship, and freedom or autonomy. In this chapter we will discuss these four candidates; then we will look at some general difficulties for pluralist views that would apply no matter what items are on the list.

5.1 Two Tests

First, though, it will be useful to think about how to evaluate potential candidates for intrinsic goods. There are many things that we want in a life, for various reasons; how do we identify the things that directly make life go better for the person living the life just in virtue of being part of that life?

One test we might apply is the "two lives" test. To apply the two lives test to some feature F, what we do is imagine two lives that are exactly identical except that one life contains F and the other lacks it. If the life with F seems better than the one without, this is some reason to think that F is a component of well-being. This test helps rule out features that are merely instrumentally good for us, such as money. If something is merely instrumentally good for us, it is good only because it leads to some other good thing, or prevents some other bad thing. So if we imagine two lives that are identical in all respects other than F, they will be identical with respect to the other good and bad things they contain. So if we judge the life with F to be better, we must think F has value independent of what it brings about; if we judge that life not to be better, then we must not think F has that sort of value.

Another way to try to figure out whether something is an element of well-being is to apply what we may call the *punishment test* (or the *reward test*) (Bentham 1962 [1789]: 77). When someone has done something bad, we might try to punish that person by doing something that would negatively impact his well-being. Conversely, we want to reward those who act well, by doing something to improve their well-being. To apply the reward/punishment test to some feature F, we ask: would it make sense to reward/punish someone for good/bad behavior by seeing to it that their life had some extra F? (Bear in mind it can't have any extra of anything else; otherwise we might be unwittingly testing for the value of that other thing!) If rewarding or punishing good or bad behavior with F makes no sense, we might doubt that F is a component of well-being. We have to be careful in using this test, though, because it often is appropriate to punish or reward someone by seeing to it that they have or lack something with merely *instrumental* value. Money is an obvious example: we reward people with monetary prizes and punish them with fines, but money is not a component of well-being. So the fact that something passes this test gives us no reason to think it is a component of well-being; only a failure could give us any useful information.

There might be other ways to determine whether something is a component of well-being. And these tests will often fail to resolve the question of whether something is a component of well-being. But they might sometimes help. Let us now look at some candidates for the pluralist's list.

5.2 Knowledge

Are we better-off just for knowing things, and are we worse off just for having false beliefs about things? If I think there are a million blades of grass in my yard, but in fact there are a million and one, am I worse off? Could my neighbor make me worse off by, unbeknownst to me, removing a blade of grass from my yard, thereby rendering one of my beliefs false (even if justified)? This may strike you as unlikely. But perhaps, just as the hedonist might try to account for objections involving worthless pleasures, the objective list theorist could try to account for worthless knowledge. Maybe some things are more worth knowing than others (Ross 1988: 145–9; Brentano 2009 [1952]: 168–70). How many blades of grass are on my lawn is not worth knowing, but the fundamental physical laws of the universe are worth knowing. Of course, the hedonist has an explanation for this: knowing the fundamental physical laws is more likely to promote happiness than knowing how many blades of grass are in my yard; it is a kind of knowledge that could be useful for all sorts of purposes, unlike knowledge of trivia. But is this the only thing that makes it worthwhile to know such things? We often behave as if we do not think so. People pursue knowledge even when they do not believe it will result in any pleasure for them or others. We donate money to universities and build expensive machines to explore outer space. Maybe we do these things for the sake of pleasure, but it is far from clear that this is so, since there are other things we could do that seem likely to promote pleasure or prevent pain more directly and effectively. Of course, you might argue that if this is so, we should be doing those other things instead; we are making a mistake in using resources the way we do. Rather than use resources to fund universities or explore space, we should be preventing suffering by donating to Oxfam and such. Since we want to make sure that we do not value knowledge merely as a means to pleasure, let us employ the two lives test. Imagine two lives that are exactly the same, except that one contains some knowledge that the other one lacks. So, for example, the two lives contain precisely the same amounts of pleasure and pain, desire fulfillments and frustrations. Is one of these lives better than the other? It seems likely there will be disagreement on this question, though when we realize that the agent has no desire to have the knowledge in question, even after she has it, it begins to seem somewhat implausible that the knowledge is good for her. Will the reward/punishment test help? Suppose we rewarded some good behavior with some knowledge. It can't be knowledge that the person wanted, or that would give the person pleasure; it's just some knowledge all by itself. Would this make sense? Perhaps some will think so; it does not seem totally absurd, but it is also not obvious that it does make sense to give someone that sort of knowledge. The two tests are not helping much. If knowledge passes them, it does not do so with flying colors.

5.3   Virtue

Virtue is a prominent candidate for the list. Plato argued in the *Republic* that the person who lacks justice cannot be happy. One of the things we care about most in raising children is seeing to it that they are good people. Perhaps this is just because we think good people are happier; but many people would want their children to be virtuous rather than vicious even if they would be slightly happier being vicious. So the view that virtue is good for the virtuous person needs to be taken seriously.

We might argue that virtue cannot be intrinsically good for us on the grounds that someone might be perfectly virtuous but be badly off. It is hard to deny that bad things happen to good people. But the pluralist need not say that one is always better-off for being virtuous. When being virtuous leads to other bad things, if those other things are bad enough, their badness might outweigh the goodness of virtue for the individual in question. Though being virtuous is intrinsically good for an individual, it can also be instrumentally bad for that individual.

When we apply the two lives test to virtue, do we get a result? If two lives are identical except that one is more virtuous – they are equally pleased, have their desires fulfilled to the same extent – is the virtuous life better for the one living it? You might choose the life with the virtue over the one without. But recall that it can be hard to be sure whether you are choosing that life for your own sake, or rather because you have an unselfish reason to choose that life, such as that it would be a better life for your family or for the world. So the two lives test is not likely to settle the question of whether virtue is intrinsically good for us.

What about the reward/punishment test? Here we seem to get a result. It seems totally inappropriate to punish someone by making him more cowardly, dishonest, or miserly. It seems similarly strange to think of rewarding someone for a good deed by making her more beneficent or honest. We might take this to be a reason to doubt that virtue and vice are components of well-being.

5.4 Friendship

When thinking about what is lost when one plugs into an experience machine, one cannot help but think about the friends and family members one would be leaving behind, never to see again. This is perhaps the most disturbing feature of the machine. This suggests that *personal relationships* are a strong candidate to be part of individual well-being. But this raises difficult questions.

Is it better to have *more* friends? In the case of other candidates for intrinsic value, it seems plausible that having more of those things is better. It is better to have more pleasure than less, for instance. But having another friend might not make things better for you. It probably depends on how many friends you already have, how good a friend the person would be, how close the friendship would be, and many other things. You might think that whether adding a friend to your life is a good idea depends on how it would affect your happiness. If you already have several close friends, you might be no happier with additional friends. It would be hard to deny that friends can be one of the most important sources of personal satisfaction and happiness in life. But remember that we are asking whether it is *intrinsically* good for you to have friends. The fact that you would be *happier* if you had more friends, or better friends, is irrelevant to this question.

Can our two tests help us here? The two lives test tells us to compare a life with friendships to a life that is identical (same amount of enjoyment, knowledge, virtue, etc.) but contains no friendships. If you think there would be no reason to prefer one of these lives to the other, then you must think that friendship is merely instrumentally good. So we might imagine that one life contains a certain amount of pleasure derived from friendship, while the other life contains the same amount of pleasure but derived from some other source, such as watching movies alone. The solitary life contains no friendship, and the life of friendship contains no movies; which is preferable? Perhaps you'd choose the life of friendship. Even so, you might deny that friendship itself is good for you; perhaps instead it is pleasure taken in friendship (recall our discussion of qualified hedonism in section 2.3).

The punishment test tells us to consider whether it would be sensible to reward good behavior by giving someone a new friend. Perhaps this strikes you as a bit odd but not absurd – why not reward someone with a friend if you could? But then we must remember that the new friend cannot increase the amount of pleasure the recipient will get. Otherwise we are not testing for the intrinsic value of friendship. So let us imagine the following scenario: God is pleased with your morally praiseworthy actions. God tells you: "I am rewarding your good behavior with a new friend named Dumpy who I created just for you. Dumpy will be your friend, but you will get no satisfaction from this friendship. Dumpy will do favors for you when asked, though you won't be any happier than you would have been if he hadn't done those favors. For example, Dumpy will help you move into your new apartment, but the amount of pain Dumpy saves you by moving things for you will be exactly counterbalanced by the additional pain you get when Dumpy drops a lamp on your toe. Dumpy will play games with you, but the enjoyment you get from playing the game will always be counterbalanced by the annoyance of Dumpy telling bad jokes. And so on. You're welcome!" Would you feel rewarded by this gift?

5.5 Freedom

Another thing people find disturbing about the experience machine is the loss of freedom or autonomy that you would endure while in the machine. You would have a series of enjoyable experiences, but you would not have control over what was happening, though you would think you did. (We could imagine a machine that did give you control; maybe that machine would seem better.) Most of us find it important to have some degree of control over what happens in our lives. To illustrate, imagine that you are handed a controller that seems to be controlling a character in a game. You do things to the controller, and the character kills monsters. You seem to be causing the character to kill the monsters, and are invested in the activity. Then you drop the controller by accident and you notice that the character is still killing the monsters, all by itself, with no help from your controller. The "controller" didn't actually do anything. You'd be disappointed and you'd think that your "controlling" actions were worthless. You'd be less invested in what the character was doing. What you thought was a fun game was actually a boring Michael Bay movie. The point is not just that you wouldn't enjoy playing with the controller anymore. Rather, when thinking about your previous activities "controlling" the character, you'd come to see that *they were not as valuable* as you previously thought, because you didn't actually have any freedom to determine what the character did.

At the risk of being tedious, let's apply our tests. Freedom passes the punishment test with flying colors. The primary way we punish people is by incarcerating them, thereby partially restricting their freedom of movement. Of course, we do that in large part for our own protection; but it does seem like a punishment nonetheless. Recall, though, that money passes the test too, so we can't conclude that freedom is intrinsically good; we can only say that it is not ruled out by this test. When we remember that the punishment can't also cause any other bad things to happen, such as frustration of desires or unhappiness, it is less clear that restricting someone's freedom, by itself, is really *punishment* rather than just protecting society. To apply the two lives test, suppose life A is just like life B except that B contains no freedom. B contains just as much happiness and desire fulfillment as A – so we have to suppose that A has no desire to act freely, and gets no additional enjoyment from her free actions. Perhaps A is still a better life than B. Rational people will disagree here, but at least freedom seems like a viable candidate, not clearly eliminated by either of our tests.

5.6 Meaningfulness

One way to describe what is missing from a life spent eating pizza and playing video games is that it is a *meaningless* existence. But what does this mean? What is it to have a meaningful life? The answers to this question have largely fallen into the same pattern as answers to the question of what it is to be well-off. Some have thought that meaningfulness is subjective – if you enjoy your life, or get what you most want in life, your life is meaningful (Taylor 2004). If this is what meaningfulness amounts to, then we have already covered it in chapters 2 and 3. More commonly, though, it is thought that there is an objective component to a meaningful life. For example, Susan Wolf has defended the view that to have a meaningful life is to have positive engagement in activities that are themselves objectively worthwhile (Wolf 2010). Since eating pizza is not objectively worthwhile in itself, a life spent eating pizza would not count as meaningful even if it were full of pleasure. Wolf's view is very similar to the more sophisticated "hybrid" versions of hedonism and desire fulfillment views discussed in chapters 2 and 3, according to which what is good for a person is to take pleasure in certain pleasure-worthy things, or to fulfill desires for objectively good things. Some have thought that achievement is of particular importance in having a meaningful life – but achievement is also alleged to be an important component of well-being (Keller 2004).

So it is not clear whether meaningfulness is really a distinct notion from well-being, and therefore not clear that meaningfulness can be a component of well-being. It might be that when someone is concerned about a lack of meaning in her life, she is really just concerned that it lacks some important component of well-being such as the ones we have already discussed. On the other hand, it might be that we could distinguish well-being and meaningfulness, and say that well-being involves enjoyment or getting what you want, while meaningfulness requires that the enjoyment be taken in objectively valuable or pleasure-worthy things.

5.7 A Problem with Lists

Suppose we find a list of good and bad things we are happy with. Our work will still not be done. For another question remains: how are the items on the list to be weighed? We must have some way to determine how well someone's life goes, given that it has some combination of those good and bad things. We will take up this problem in the next chapter.

There is a feature of pluralism that many have found troubling: whatever list of good things we come up with, why are these things, rather than some other things, on the list? This question cannot, in principle, be answered by pluralism. There's just a list; that's the end of the story. If there were an answer to why these things were on the list, that answer would provide a unifying theory, which is the thing the pluralist rejects. This makes it seem like the pluralist is not really answering the question we began this book with. We wanted an explanation of why some things are good for us and others are not. The pluralist does not seem to provide such an explanation.

But is this a problem for pluralism? According to Roger Crisp there is a difference between "enumerative" and "explanatory" theories of well-being (Crisp 2006: 102–3). An enumerative theory tells us *which* things are good for us; an explanatory theory tells us *why* those things are good for us. Pluralism would count as an enumerative theory, because it tells us *which* things are good for us. It would not count as an explanatory theory, because it does not tell us *why* those things are on the list. There isn't any further explanation of why those things are on the list. We might take it as a defect of pluralism that it does not count as explanatory. But Crisp's distinction is ultimately not very helpful in identifying a special problem for pluralism relative to other theories. Once we arrive at a fundamentally good thing, the only explanation of what it is that makes that thing good for us is *that it is the sort of thing that it is*. This is so whether it is the only fundamentally good thing or just one of several. Thus, as Crisp says, "the hedonist...will say that what makes accomplishment, enjoyable experiences, or whatever good for people is *their being enjoyable*" (Crisp 2006: 103). We can say something similar about the other items on the pluralist's list. What makes a belief good for people is *it being knowledge*, and so on.

The pluralist will point out that explanation must stop somewhere; where explanation stops, the pluralist finds more than one thing. We should not look for deeper unity where there is none to be found; there is no "essence" to well-being beyond its consisting of this list of things. She might also point out that hedonism is not in an obviously better position on this score: why is only this one thing, pleasure, on the good list? The hedonist can't answer this question either. Perhaps the objection to pluralism relies on the natural thought that, for certain sorts of things at least, the question "how many of these things are there?" has some answers that seem less arbitrary than others. Zero, one, and infinitely many are non-arbitrary-seeming answers; three, eight, and 745,982 are arbitrary-seeming answers.[6] But this depends on the sort of thing we are talking about. It is not arbitrary to

---

[6] Compare David Lewis's discussion of possible sizes of spacetime (Lewis 1986: 103).

say there are two kinds of elephant or 1,467,358,448 kinds of insect. That's just how many there are (let's say). We figured it out by counting them. Maybe we can just count up the intrinsic goods, and find out that there are five kinds. But is this a sufficient reply on behalf of pluralism? The fact that there are two kinds of elephant is not a brute, inexplicable fact. Evolutionary biologists can tell us a story about why there are two kinds of elephant. But if there are exactly five sorts of things that are good for a person, this is, on the pluralist's story, a brute, inexplicable fact about the universe. Depending on your philosophical temperament, you may find it hard to believe that such a thing could be inexplicable.[7]

5.8 Further Reading

Chapters V and VI of W.D. Ross's *The Right and the Good* (1988) make a good starting point for thinking about pluralism, even though he is discussing intrinsic goodness rather than well-being. For some recent versions of pluralism, see Jean Kazez (2007), John Finnis (2011), James Griffin (1986) and Thomas Hurka (2011). On the connection between virtue and well-being, see Julia Annas (1998), Paul Bloomfield (2014), Brad Hooker (1996) and ch. 8 of Haybron (2008). On autonomy or freedom, see Kazez (2007). On meaningfulness, Susan Wolf's *Meaning in Life and Why it Matters* (2010) and Thaddeus Metz's *Meaning in Life* (2013) are some important recent works. Related to Bentham's punishment test, see Brad Hooker's "Sympathy Test" (1996: 149–55). See Franz Brentano's *Foundation and Construction of Ethics* (2009 [1952]: 166) for a criticism of Bentham's punishment test.

---

[7] Thanks to Chris Heathwood for discussion of this thought.

6
Aggregating and Measuring Well-Being

We have discussed many views about the constituents of well-being. But many interesting questions about well-being remain. In this chapter we will consider two sorts of questions. (1) How is well-being aggregated? Here there are two sub-questions: (1a) How do the constituents of well-being go together to determine how well an individual's life goes? (1b) How do we get the well-being of a *group* of people, the general welfare, from the welfare of the individuals in the group? (2) How can well-being be measured? Naturally the answer to this second question will depend on what the constituents of well-being are. We will look at how well-being is actually being measured by social scientists, and see what presuppositions they are making about the constituents of well-being.

6.1 Aggregating Different Kinds of Goods

The pluralist thinks there is more than one kind of thing that is good for us. Suppose that pleasure, knowledge, and virtue are the three components of well-being. How do we determine how well someone's life goes on the basis of these three components? Are they all equally important, and what would it mean to say that one is more important than another?

A simple thought is just to add up the values of the items on the list. For example, if Joe gets 10 units of pleasure, and 10 units of knowledge, and 10 units of virtue, his life would have a value of 30 for him. But how are the "units" to be determined across types of value? The choice of unit will be doing all the work here. The question of how to weigh the items on the list merely gets reformulated as the question of how to determine what counts as one unit of each sort of thing. As an analogy, suppose we want to know how "big" something is, but we have two components of "bigness": volume and mass. Suppose we said that to determine how big something is, we just sum units of volume and units of mass. Then the units we choose will determine whether one thing is bigger than another. If we choose a cubic centimeter as our unit of volume and a kilogram as our unit of mass, A might count as bigger than B, while if our units are the cubic kilometer and the gram, B might count as bigger than A. The choice of unit is arbitrary. That arbitrariness makes no difference as long as we are comparing volume with volume, or mass with mass. But it makes a big difference when we compare volume with mass. This is the problem the pluralist about well-being faces. The arbitrariness of the choice of an amount of pleasure to count as one hedon makes no difference when comparing amounts of pleasure, but makes a big difference when comparing amounts of pleasure to amounts of knowledge.

To avoid worries about comparing units, we might say that the components of well-being can be given a *lexical ordering*. For example, suppose that there are only two goods: pleasure and knowledge. We might think that pleasure *always* outweighs knowledge. When comparing two possible lives, we first look at which one contains more pleasure. If one contains more pleasure, then it is better. If they are equal in pleasure, we then look at which one contains more knowledge; the one that contains more knowledge would be better. But this is very implausible; if knowledge really impacts well-being, how could it be that a tiny bit of pleasure could outweigh an enormous amount of knowledge? Since the amounts of pleasure in any two lives would almost never be identical, knowledge would effectively have little or no impact on well-being.

If there is no lexical ordering, what determines the relative values of the good things? This question might be impossible to answer for the pluralist. But once again, the hedonist has a similar problem: how can the positive values of pleasures and the negative values of pains be compared? Pleasure and pain are distinct feelings, and it is not clear how to compare one combination of pleasure and pain with another. Perhaps the only view that gets around this problem is the desire fulfillment view. If what is good for an individual is getting what she wants, and what is bad is not getting what she wants, the goodness of getting what one wants and the badness of not getting what one wants may both be determined by the same thing: the degree of desire.

6.2   Aggregating Well-Being Within a Life

Let us put aside the worries of the previous section and assume, for simplicity's sake, that pleasure is the only fundamental intrinsic good, that pain is the only fundamental intrinsic evil, and that pleasures and pains can be compared, so that the absolute value of one hedon (unit of pleasure) is identical to the absolute value of one dolor (unit of pain). If we want to figure out how well someone's whole life goes, the simplest thing to do would be to add up the values of the pleasures and pains in it (where pains have negative values).

But perhaps this way of aggregating is too simple. Imagine a life that begins in destitution and pain, but gradually gets better and better, until the last years of life are intensely happy. Now imagine a life that begins with great happiness and success, but slowly deteriorates until the person dies miserable and penniless. Suppose that, if we just added up the values of the pleasures and pains in these lives, the sums would be identical. You still might not think that the lives are equally good; you might think the improving life is better than the declining one (Chisholm 1986: 70–1; Glasgow 2013).

If you think these things, then you think that lives are what has been called "organic unities." The value of a life is not equal to the sum of the values of its parts. The relations between the parts also matter in determining how well a life goes.

Of course, it is controversial whether improvement makes a difference to how well a life goes. You might prefer the improving life because you think that while living it, you would have some additional enjoyment or satisfaction in anticipating future goods, while if you were in the declining life you would have additional disappointments relating to your life's trajectory.

Suppose you think that it is good for a life to improve, even if the amount of enjoyment or fulfillment in the improving life is no greater than in the declining life. You may still wonder *why* improvement matters. One view is that it is just an inexplicable fact that improvement is better. But it would be nice to be able to say why it is better. One thought is that improvement is better because (and only when) the later goods are appropriately related to the prior misfortunes, as when one learns from one's misfortunes and uses that knowledge to improve one's future, or when the prior misfortune in some other way is responsible for the later benefits. As an example, consider the following scenario (Velleman 1993: 337–8). A man is deciding, after some marital difficulties and therapy, whether to stay with his spouse or start over with someone new. If he stays with his spouse, he will be slightly less happy than he would be if he started over with someone new. But the goods in his life will be redeeming his past struggles; he will be building on his past rather than throwing it away. If he were to start over with a new spouse, his future would not be connected to his past in this way; it would not be a story of redeemed sacrifice, but of vain sacrifice. Or consider a different scenario: two women have great financial success, but the success of one is the result of her hard work in her job, while the other just wins the lottery. The life story in which success is the payoff from hard work is a better story than the story in which success is just randomly bestowed. If we thought that the value of a life was just determined by adding the values of its parts, we would not be able to see any importance in redeeming past sacrifices or suffering; and if we thought that it was just a brute fact that improvement was good, we would not be able to say that it is better to redeem past sacrifices than to have a lucky windfall.

Whether it makes sense to redeem past misfortunes raises interesting questions about well-being. It is natural to think that what we should be worried about is how well-off we will be in the future. But if it makes sense to redeem past misfortunes, then it is not just future well-being that should concern us; rather, we should care about *global features* of our lives, and how our future will relate to our past. Sometimes, this could require us to choose a suboptimal future in light of the fact that it fits better with our past than the better future does. For example, suppose you have devoted the last three years of your life to becoming a painter. It has involved a lot of work and sacrifice on your part. You *could* continue on and become a painter, making your years of effort pay off. On the other hand, you could take a government job, and you would be slightly happier in the future if you took that job. If you should care about global features of your life, you should keep trying to become a painter even though you would be happier in the future if you quit. You might find that surprising.

Many people also seem to think that what happens at the end of a life plays a more important role in determining how well the life goes than what happens at other times. Psychologist Ed Diener has called this the "James Dean Effect" (Diener et al. 2001). Imagine two lives. The first life (which we might imagine to be, in some respects, relevantly like James Dean's life) is very happy throughout but ends at age 30. The second is just like the first for the first 30 years, but contains an additional ten years of moderate happiness at the end. According to a study conducted by Diener and colleagues, most people seem to think that the shorter life is better. But of course if we add up the moments of happiness in the two lives, the second must be better. Perhaps this shows that the quality of the *end* period of life plays an outsized role in our judgments about the quality of the life overall. This would be another sort of organic unity.

Again, we might wonder whether, upon reflection, we should accept the judgment that the shorter life is better. Maybe it just makes for a better story, but doesn't make the life better for the person living it. And if it is really better to have the shorter life, wouldn't it therefore be *prudent* to commit suicide at your peak? This does not seem right.

Here is another sort of case that might make you believe in organic unities (Parfit 1986: 160). First, imagine the most fortunate life that anyone has ever actually lived. Let's suppose it is a very long and happy life – it lasts 100 years and contains an average of 100 hedons per day, for a total of about 3,650,000 hedons. Probably nobody has ever been so happy; maybe this is a much more fortunate life than anyone has ever lived. Now imagine a life that contains a very small amount of pleasure each day, and always the same sort of pleasure. Perhaps the individual enjoys a cheeseburger each day, and gets one hedon from each cheeseburger. Imagine that due to life-extending technology, this life lasts for *1,000,000 years*. If the value of the life equals the sum of the values of the parts, then since the person gets a hedon each day for about 365,000,000 days, this life would be at least one hundred times better than the most fortunate life that anyone has ever lived. You might think this is absurd. Just making a life longer wouldn't make it so much better. A life of normal length that contained such a great amount of pleasure each day would be much better than the perpetual mild pleasures offered by the cheeseburger life.

Maybe you would prefer the shorter life in this case because you think that after a few years of cheeseburgers, you would be really bored of cheeseburgers; in that case you wouldn't actually be getting a hedon from all of those cheeseburgers. You might even be getting dolors. (There is some evidence that this does not happen with donuts, though!; Frederick and Loewenstein 1999: 314.) Adding up the values of these hedons and dolors would not give us a very high number; we might get the right result after all. But suppose you wouldn't get bored; perhaps you have a short-term memory and don't remember the previous cheeseburgers. Would the cheeseburger life be better in that case? If you don't think so, then you might think the cheeseburger life is another example of an organic unity: the value of the whole does not equal the sum of the values of the parts. The value of the whole is less than the sum of the values of the parts.

There are different explanations you might give for what is going on here. Perhaps variety matters in itself; having a repeated cheeseburger pleasure might be less valuable than having different kinds of pleasures (see Chisholm 1986: 70–1 on Brentano's principle of "bonum variationis"). Or perhaps the problem is that the cheeseburger pleasure is a "lower" pleasure (2.5), and lower pleasures do not aggregate in the way that "higher" pleasures do; additional lower pleasures do not make things better for you to the same extent that higher pleasures would. Recall what Mill says about this topic in *Utilitarianism*:

> If one of the two [pleasures] is, by those who are competently acquainted with both, placed so far above the other that they prefer it, even though knowing it to be attended with a greater amount of discontent, and would not resign it for any quantity of the other pleasure which their nature is capable of, we are justified in ascribing to the preferred enjoyment a superiority in quality so far outweighing quantity as to render it, in comparison, of small account. (1861: 12)

Mill suggests that there are some pleasures, lower pleasures, that simply could not add up in value to the value of a higher pleasure no matter how much of it there was (as long as it is an amount "their nature is capable of"). Mill might say that the cheeseburger pleasures aren't adding up to all that much value.

Maybe, though, it is just a mistake to prefer the shorter life to the longer one. Think about how much longer you'd live! It is hard to grasp what it would be like to live for a million years; if you really did grasp it, and how much more total enjoyment it would contain, maybe you'd prefer that life to a life of normal length with pleasures crammed more tightly into it.

6.3   Aggregating Well-Being Across Lives

Sometimes we want to aggregate well-being not just within a life, but across lives. We might want to know, for example, what would most benefit our country. If we want to figure out how things are going in a population, should we just add up the well-being levels of the individuals there?

In order to add up well-being levels of different people, *interpersonal well-being level comparison* must be possible.

You might doubt whether it is. Supposing pleasure is intrinsically good for us, how can we know how much pleasure someone is getting? In the next section we will look at how social scientists attempt to figure this out. But it is clearly not easy. A non-invasive way would be to ask people how pleased they are. But suppose we ask two people how pleased they are on a scale of 1 to 10. One might say "4" and the other might say "7." But that might be only because one is more optimistic than the other about what other pleasures might be available to him in the future, and might therefore be leaving more room for pleasures to be better than what he is currently getting. The two might actually be feeling very similar pleasures. How could we tell whether this was the case? We might hook them up to machines so we could see what was happening in their brains. But that itself would interfere with how much pleasure they were getting. It is unpleasant being hooked up to a machine. Perhaps we will develop ways to scan a brain from a distance, so as not to interfere with the subject's enjoyment. Still, it is unclear how what we detect when we inspect someone's brain corresponds to the amount of pleasure the person is feeling. Even if we know which parts of the brain to look at to detect whether someone is experiencing pleasure, would we have any reason to think that brain-state B1 involves, say, *twice as much pleasure* as brain-state B2? We might try to figure this out by asking people how pleased they are and observing their brain-state at that time, and noting that when someone is in B1 they claim to be experiencing twice as much pleasure as when they are in B2; but appeals to self-reports reintroduce the previous difficulty. Finally, suppose that pleasure is not a distinct feeling at all, but an attitude; in that case, someone might be pleased that something is the case without there being anything interesting happening in the "pleasure centers" of her brain. It is not hard to see that, for other components of well-being, similar problems may arise in trying to measure them.

Is this really a problem? We need to distinguish the *practical* problem, how to actually figure out how much pleasure someone is feeling, from the *theoretical* problem, whether there is any fact of the matter about how much pleasure someone is feeling. We might never solve the practical problem, but that would not show that there is no fact of the matter about how much pleasure someone is feeling – just that we will never know the answer. It is, however, difficult to say with great confidence that there is a fact of the matter about how much pleasure someone is feeling if we have no way to figure out what that amount is. (We'll return to measurement questions shortly.)

If we can compare well-being levels between people, we can attempt to figure out how well-off a population is on the basis of how well its members are. We might think that one population is better-off than another if it has a greater total amount of well-being. But there are reasons to doubt this. Consider two populations. In P1, there are a *billion extremely well-off people*. Each of those people is living a life that is as good as any life you know about. In P2, everyone is barely well-off – each has a life that is just barely worth living, containing, say, just one hedon – but there are many more than a billion people. As long as there are enough people in P2, when we sum their well-being levels, the total will be greater than the total amount of well-being in P1. Yet intuitively, P1 seems to be better-off than P2. It does not seem we can make a very large and well-off population better-off just by making it *bigger* – but that would be possible, if the well-being of a population is determined by summing the well-being levels of the members of the population.

If, instead of summing the well-being of the members of a population, we *average* their well-being levels, we avoid this problem. P1 has a much higher average well-being level than P2. When social psychologists measure the subjective well-being levels of countries, they are interested in average levels – they would not say that India and China are the happiest countries just because there is more total well-being there due to the large number of people who live there. But we might wonder about the average view, too. Suppose that population P3 has 100 moderately well-off people. P4 has 99 unhappy people plus George, who is extraordinarily well-off. George is so well-off that when you calculate the average well-being levels of P3 and P4, P4's average is higher even though everyone in P3 is better-off than all the non-George members of P4. You might wonder whether that really means that P4 is better-off than P3.

Perhaps it would be better to look at the *median* level of well-being. P3 has a higher median level than P4. But this view is probably not an improvement. If the well-being level of a population is determined by its median well-being level, then improving the well-being level of people above the median, without affecting anyone else's well-being, will have no impact on the well-being of the population. Even more implausibly, *decreasing* the well-being level of people *below* the median will not make the population worse off! That cannot be right.

If we want to insist that a change to anyone's well-being affects the well-being of a population, and we don't want to say that merely adding some well-off people to a population always makes that population better-off, then we are led back to the average view. We can explain away the thought that P3 is better-off than P4 by noting that there are two very similar, but distinct, questions we can ask about the distribution of well-being in a population. In addition to wanting to know how the distribution of well-being in a population affects *how well-off* the population is, we might want to know *how good it is* to distribute well-being in one way rather than another. The value of a distribution might be determined by something other than how well-off it makes the population. Thus although P4 is better-off than P3, P3 has a better distribution of well-being than P4, so we should prefer the distribution in P3 to the distribution in P4. In chapter 7 we will address the question of what determines the value of a distribution of well-being.

6.4   Measuring Well-Being

Recently there has been a great deal of empirical research into well-being. The results of this research can be used to influence policy; for example, the country of Bhutan has placed happiness at the core of its national policy, evaluating policies in terms of their effects on the "Gross National Happiness." It is important, therefore, to understand this research and what it shows.

As we have already seen at great length, there are many unresolved fundamental questions about well-being. There is no philosophical consensus about the nature of well-being, about what constitutes well-being, or about what determines the well-being of a population. What, then, are these empirical studies measuring?

The most prevalent sort of empirical research into well-being consists of conducting surveys where participants are asked a question like: taking all things into account, how happy or satisfied are you with your life these days? (Recall the "whole-life satisfaction view" of well-being from chapter 2.) Thus participants are intended to provide a global judgment of their lives, rather than just reporting how they feel at the moment. The judgment is subjective: it is an expression of the *participant's attitude or feelings* about his or her life. Thus these researchers take themselves to be measuring what they call "subjective well-being" (SWB for short).

Psychologists Diener and Lucas explain one of the assumptions behind this research as follows: "In the assessment of SWB, researchers make a critical assumption about the nature of self-reports of happiness: when an individual says he or she has high SWB, this report reflects (albeit imperfectly) a state with some temporal stability and is not the reflection of a capricious decision resulting from momentary factors only" (Diener and Lucas 1999: 213–14). This assumption seems to be called into question by some empirical studies. One very early study purported to show that current weather conditions play a strong role in determining reports of subjective well-being: those who participated on sunny days reported higher satisfaction with life than those who participated on rainy days (Schwarz and Clore 1983). If subjective well-being reports are so greatly influenced by transitory circumstances like whether it is sunny outside, this would call into question whether there is really a stable mental state underlying those reports.[8] But a recent and much larger study by Lucas and Lawless has shown no connection between weather conditions and SWB reports (Lucas and Lawless 2013). Thus some of these early studies are called into serious question. The

[8] Yardley and Rice (1991) argue that well-being could be fairly stable and yet also depend partly on transitory factors.

bulk of research now suggests that subjective well-being is actually a fairly stable phenomenon – reports of subjective well-being tend not to change drastically from day to day, and a person's well-being reports tend to correlate with what other people think about whether that person is well-off.[9] This is not to say that well-being is impervious to changes in life situation. Individuals who lose a loved one report decreases in well-being that can last a significant length of time; losing a job also has long-lasting negative effects (Luhmann et al. 2012). But if well-being reports were *drastically* affected by *trivial* events or circumstances, perhaps we would have reason to doubt that there is a significant phenomenon being measured by SWB research. At least, that is the assumption. But then again we might wonder why SWB must be stable (Feldman 2010: 77). Why can't SWB vary significantly from moment to moment? This might make SWB more difficult to measure, but it would not make it any less real.

In light of the first several chapters of this book, we should first note that, since SWB research purports to measure only *subjective* well-being, it is not clear that it measures well-being at all. Consider, for example, how someone would respond to a SWB survey if he believed that his family and "friends" loved him, and felt very good about this, but they secretly hated him and betrayed him. Such a person would likely report that his life was going extremely well. But you might think that things are not really going very well for him even though he thinks they are. Consider, also, that you might not know, concerning many of your most important desires, whether they will be satisfied or not. If a desire fulfillment view were true, *you would have no idea* of how well things are going for you. So your answers to a SWB survey would indicate very little about your well-being. Similar things might be said concerning perfectionist and pluralist theories of well-being: if some such theory is true, whether you are well-off would have little to do with what you think about it, and you might not be in a very good position to know how well-off you are. As Valerie Tiberius points out, "while objective accounts are mainstream in philosophy, they are somewhat

[9] For a summary of these findings, see Diener and Lucas (1999), 214–15.

on the fringe of psychological work on well-being" (Tiberius 2006: 495).

It is important to keep this disconnect between psychological and philosophical approaches to well-being in mind, but we should not belabor it. Philosophers have been attempting for millennia to come up with a true theory of well-being, and there is little reason to think consensus is just around the corner. Social scientists cannot wait for philosophy to sort out this question. SWB seems like it is at least *relevant* to well-being, whether or not it is the whole story. Even if some objective theory of well-being is true, SWB reports might be a good *indicator* of well-being, as long as people tend to be satisfied with their lives when they have whatever objective features of a life really make it good for them, such as freedom or friendship. At the same time, we must be aware of the dangers inherent in focusing on subjective well-being reports. For example, we risk overestimating the well-being of oppressed people whose preferences have adapted (see section 3.4).

6.5 The Causes of Well-Being

Several studies indicate that we are not always good judges of our own subjective well-being. A famous study of colonoscopy patients by Redelmeier and Kahneman seems to show that people misjudge the value of their experience; their judgments are unduly influenced by the last part of the experience, so that an experience that clearly contains more pain is judged better than one that contains less if the end of the procedure is less painful (Redelmeier and Kahneman 1996). Other studies seem to show that we are unrealistically optimistic about various aspects of our lives. Taylor and Brown claim that "the mentally healthy person may not be fully cognizant of the day-to-day flotsam and jetsam of life. Rather, the mentally healthy person appears to have the enviable capacity to distort reality" (Taylor and Brown 1988). These positive illusions seem likely to extend to SWB reports.

David Benatar argues that in light of this, we have good reason to think that our lives are not nearly as good as we think, and that in fact we would all be better-off never to have been born at all. We forget most of the times we are itchy, or hungry, or too hot, or too cold (Benatar 2006: 71–3). If we accurately remembered these experiences, we would not find our lives to be worth living; our subjective well-being reports would be much more negative. If Benatar were correct, the implications would be enormous. We would seem to have very strong reasons never to procreate, for example, since we would always be creating people with poor lives. We would also seem to have reason to see to it that all sentient life on Earth comes to a (painless) end as soon as possible, since sentience is on balance bad for everyone.[10]

Here it is useful to know that some psychologists, including Daniel Kahneman, have attempted to measure well-being episodically – and in fact these measurements are what enable us to know that people's memories of their colonoscopies are inaccurate. Rather than asking how things are going these days, subjects in Kahneman's studies of "objective happiness" are asked about their current hedonic state (Kahneman 1999). If Benatar were correct, then we would expect these reports to be very negative. People would be reporting that they currently are displeased because they are hungry, or itchy, or hot, or cold. But (as far as I can tell) no studies of episodic well-being have shown any such thing. Perhaps our lives are not as good as we remember, but insofar as their value is determined by subjective feelings, they are still well worth living, both for the healthy and fortunate and, in most cases, for the disabled and traumatized.

Supposing that subjectively worthwhile lives are possible and even widespread, we may wish to know how to go about living such a life. There is so much research relevant to this question currently being done that it is difficult to keep up with the findings. This research has the potential to have great implications for how we should live our lives if we want to be happy, and what policies we should adopt if we want society to be happy. It would not be possible to discuss all

[10] Benatar also has a separate argument for the claim that it is better never to have been born, based on a conceptual asymmetry between pleasure and pain (Benatar 2006: ch. 2). I criticize this argument in Bradley (2010).

the potential effects on well-being here. But one general question is worth discussing: how much of an impact on our well-being can we expect to have?

Using SWB as a benchmark for policy presupposes that adopting different policies can affect how well-off people are. This is certainly true for some policies. Adopting a policy of torturing people whenever possible would obviously have a negative impact on a society's well-being. We do not need to take surveys to figure this out. But the kinds of policies we are normally called on to evaluate, such as taxation policies, do not have such obvious impacts. Similarly, if you make your decisions about what to do based on what will make you happier, you are supposing that your choices will affect your SWB.

There are some reasons to think that the effects of these choices on our well-being are limited. One reason is that your *personality* and your *genes* seem to have a big influence on your SWB (Diener and Lucas 1999). How extroverted or neurotic you are is strongly correlated with the degree of satisfaction you will report with your life, and twins raised in separate households report very similar SWB (Diener and Lucas 1999: 216–19). Most of the decisions you make are not going to affect your personality, and none will affect your genetic makeup; thus they will have only limited impact on your SWB. Likewise, most policy decisions will not affect the personalities of the people affected, and thus their effects on the SWB of the general population will be limited.

Another reason is what is widely called the "hedonic treadmill" or "hedonic adaptation" (Frederick and Loewenstein 1999). When something good or bad happens to us, we may have some short-term happiness or unhappiness; but over time we tend to return to, or near, our prior levels of happiness. For example, people often think their lives would be terrible if they were to become disabled. But there is no evidence that this is generally the case. People who become disabled do tend to go through a period of diminished happiness, but happiness levels rise again, and depending on the specific disability, can approach their pre-disability levels (Frederick and Loewenstein 1999: 312). People also often misjudge what the effects of achieving a goal or fulfilling a desire will be on their subjective well-being. You might think:

*if I just get this promotion, or this raise, or if I get this car
that I want, I'll finally be happy.* But this is not generally
true. A famous study of lottery winners shows that they are
not generally happier after winning than other people.[11] Mar-
riage and divorce seem to have little or no lasting effect on
SWB (Luhmann et al. 2012). In general, the moral of much
of the current psychological research on subjective well-being
is that life events of many sorts do not have as much impact
on our well-being as we think they do.

Sometimes these kinds of mistakes can have important
implications. If you know that winning the lottery cannot be
expected to make you happier, then you should probably stop
wasting your money. More importantly, mistakes you make
about the well-being of the disabled might affect your procreative decisions in the event you discover that your unborn
child will have a disability. You might have thought that this
means your child would be unhappy; but this is probably not
true. The moral of this discussion is not that you should stop
trying to affect your (and others') SWB altogether; we do not
have evidence that SWB is *impervious* to external factors. The
point is rather that you should temper your expectations
about the extent to which life events will make you happier,
given that at least some things that you might have thought
would be likely to make you happy or unhappy do not in
fact generally have that effect.

6.6   Further Reading

On comparing different kinds of goods, see Ruth Chang (ed.),
Incommensurability, Incomparability, and Practical Reason
(1998). For an example of a lexical view, see W.D. Ross's
The Right and the Good (1988, ch. VI; Ross is concerned
with goodness *simpliciter* rather than well-being but the
issues are the same). On aggregating goods within a life, an
influential paper has been David Velleman's "Well-Being and

---

[11] See Brickman et al. (1978). It is worth noting that the number of
lottery winners studied was only 22. Thus we should not be sur-
prised if a larger study showed different results.

Time" (1993). See chapter 6 of Feldman (2004) for a defense of hedonism against such arguments. On aggregating goods across lives, there is an enormous literature on what Derek Parfit calls the "repugnant conclusion" (1984: ch. 17). This problem was first noticed by Sidgwick in *The Methods of Ethics* (1907: 414–16), but Parfit's discussion is an excellent starting point for thinking about these issues. See Jesper Ryberg and Torbjörn Tännsjö (eds.), *The Repugnant Conclusion* (2004), for a good collection of recent work. On measuring well-being, there is an even more enormous literature. A good starting place is Kahneman, Diener and Schwarz's *Well-Being: The Foundations of Hedonic Psychology* (1999). For philosophical discussions of this literature and good discussions of the relationship between the science and philosophy of well-being, see Dan Haybron (2008), Valerie Tiberius (2006, 2013), Anna Alexandrova (2011, 2012), and Fred Feldman (2010).

7

Well-Being and Normative Theory

Well-being is an important concept in normative ethics and public policy. According to **welfarism**, facts about well-being are wholly responsible for determining what we ought to do, how resources should be distributed, what laws we should have, and so on. Welfarism has a good deal of initial plausibility. For example, laws against homosexual behavior can be convincingly criticized on the grounds that such laws negatively affect some people's well-being without making anyone better-off; that these criticisms seem compelling gives us reason to think that welfarism is plausible. Welfarism is a powerful antidote to entrenched traditional values that have outlived their usefulness. Welfarism underlies the grandfather of normative ethical theories: utilitarianism. We'll begin this chapter with a discussion of utilitarianism, and then move on to discuss views that give well-being a less dominant role.

7.1 Utilitarianism

Utilitarianism is a theory in the normative ethics of behavior. The primary goal of normative ethics is to provide a criterion of morally permissible behavior: to say what it is that makes an action morally permissible. (Sometimes we say that we are interested in what makes an action morally "right" – see, for example, the quotation from Mill below. But the term "right" has multiple meanings and sometimes seems to be synonymous with "obligatory," so I use the term "permissible" to avoid confusion.) Given a criterion of morally permissible behavior, we can say what makes an action morally wrong or morally obligatory. To say that an action is morally *wrong* is to say that it would not be morally permissible to do it; to say that an action is morally *obligatory* is to say that it would be morally wrong not to do it. *Moral* permissibility is to be distinguished from other sorts of permissibility, such as *legal* permissibility. Whether an action is legally permissible can be determined by consulting the law of the land. But sometimes we know that an act is permitted by the law of the land, but still wish to criticize the act; and sometimes we know an act is legally forbidden but we think that in an important sense it still ought to be done. In such cases, we are most interested in the moral status of the act, not its legal status.

Utilitarianism, then, is a criterion of morally permissible behavior. John Stuart Mill famously states utilitarianism as follows:

> The creed which accepts as the foundation of morals "utility" or the "greatest happiness principle" holds that actions are right in proportion as they tend to promote happiness; wrong as they tend to produce the reverse of happiness. By happiness is intended pleasure and the absence of pain; by unhappiness, pain and the privation of pleasure. (Mill 1861: 10)

Mill's statement of utilitarianism builds in some features that would be contentious among utilitarians. First, there is the phrase "in proportion," which suggests that moral rightness or permissibility comes in degrees. While there may be good reason to desire a moral theory that ranks actions in this way, we might also want to know whether a particular action is morally permissible full stop. Mill's statement does not help us with this. Second, there is the term "tends," which suggests that an act may generally promote happiness but sometimes not. This makes sense only if we are evaluating a type of action, rather than a particular action performed by a particular person on some occasion, or an act "token." So Mill's statement does not help us if we want to evaluate an act token, which we often do.

To formulate utilitarianism more carefully, let us introduce some terminology. Let us say that the hedonic utility of an action is the total amount of pleasure it produces minus the total amount of pain it produces (here we will rely on our assumptions about pleasure and pain from chapter 2). Let us also say that a particular action maximizes hedonic utility if and only if no alternative action that could be performed in the situation would produce more hedonic utility. Utilitarianism, then, will be stated as follows:

HU: An act is morally permissible if and only if it maximizes hedonic utility.

HU does a good job of capturing a Millian strand of utilitarian thought, but we might want to formulate utilitarianism even more broadly. After all, we have seen throughout the course of this book that most philosophers reject hedonism. And if hedonism is false then HU is surely false, for why would we be obligated to maximize hedonic utility if something other than pleasure is intrinsically good for people? So let us not presuppose the truth of any particular theory of well-being, and instead formulate utilitarianism as follows:

U: An act is morally permissible if and only if it maximizes well-being.

U has a good deal of initial plausibility. It offers a straightforward explanation of the fact that it is morally wrong to inflict pain on other people or animals – such actions cause a decrease in well-being. Well-being is something we all care about, so U explains moral permissibility in terms of something important to us. If you think well-being is all that fundamentally matters for morality, then U probably most clearly encapsulates your view of morality.

Is it morally impermissible to *fail to maximize* well-being? There are several sorts of examples that make this seem implausible. Many have found U too demanding. Maybe sometimes it is permissible to do something that is less than the very best thing with respect to well-being; maybe it is permissible to "satisfice," or perform an action that is "good enough." For example, maybe it is permissible to give only $1,000 to Oxfam, even though you could afford to give $2,000, and even though if you gave $2,000, more well-being would be produced. Giving $1,000 is good enough and therefore morally permissible. Even if this is true, it would not impact the *welfarist* presupposition of U. Well-being would still be all that fundamentally matters; we would just have more latitude with respect to our moral obligations concerning well-being.

Recall our discussion of the "Repugnant Conclusion" in section 6.3. Imagine that you can bring about a future with a billion extremely well-off people. Suppose you have another alternative: bring about a future with people who are barely well-off, but there are many more people. As long as there are enough people, when we sum their well-being levels, the total will be greater than the total amount of well-being of the billion extremely well-off people. U apparently entails that you should bring about the future with the barely well-off people. But as we saw in section 6.3, this depends on how we aggregate well-being. If the value of an outcome is determined by how many well-off people are there, and how well-off a group of people is depends on the average well-being of the members rather than the total well-being (as seemed to be the most plausible view about the well-being of a population), then the better outcome is the one with the billion extremely well-off people, and U requires you to bring about that outcome. If an averaging view is plausible, then the Repugnant Conclusion is not an objection to welfarism.

However, it is not clear that we can save welfarism by appeal to an averaging view. Here is a clever argument due to Derek Parfit (1984: ch. 19). If we accept welfarism and an averaging view of the welfare of a population, then we must reject another plausible principle, called the Mere Addition Principle (MAP). According to the MAP, merely adding a well-off person to a population (without thereby affecting anyone else's well-being) does not make things worse. Suppose we have a population of very happy people and we can add another very happy, but somewhat less happy person to the population. The MAP tells us that this would at least not make things *worse*. But welfarism plus the averaging view tells us that it would make things worse, because it reduces the average welfare of the population. Rejecting MAP seems like a high cost to pay to preserve welfarism.

Other solutions to the Repugnant Conclusion require us to attribute value to something other than well-being, such as justice (on the assumption that those in the barely well-off population are getting less than they deserve to get in life) (Feldman 1995). If some such solution to the Repugnant Conclusion is required, then welfarism is not true.

There are other sorts of cases where it seems more clear that well-being is not all that matters in our moral evaluations of actions. For example, suppose the rest of the class would benefit by harming one student, Joe. Perhaps they would enjoy seeing Joe kicked in the shins. Joe has done nothing to deserve this. It would hurt Joe to be kicked. Nevertheless, if the other students got enough enjoyment from seeing Joe kicked, and if there are enough students in the class, their enjoyment might outweigh Joe's suffering. Yet that does not make it permissible to kick Joe. If this is so, then something in addition to well-being is relevant to what we ought to do. In this case, we might explain why Joe cannot be kicked by saying that in addition to how much well-being is produced by an action, *how that well-being is distributed* makes an important difference. In particular, it makes a difference whether the well-being is distributed *fairly*. It is unfair to abuse Joe to benefit others, and this makes it impermissible. Or we might say that Joe has a *right* not to be made worse off, even if this would maximize well-being for humanity at large.

Another well-known objection involves promises (Ross 1988: 17–18). If I have promised to benefit X, but I could benefit Y slightly more by breaking my promise, U entails that I should break my promise (assuming there is nothing else better I could do). But surely the fact that I made a promise is relevant to what I am morally permitted to do. This is not to say that I am always morally required to keep my promises, no matter the consequences; but the fact that I have made a promise provides a weighty moral reason to keep it, and a small increase in the total welfare that could be produced by breaking the promise is not sufficient to outweigh the weighty reason in favor of keeping promises.

There are ways of improving a person's well-being that seem to interfere too much in that person's ability to determine her own fate. Think of the "angel of death" who painlessly murders people who are terminally ill and suffering but prefer not to die; even if the murderer improves the well-being of his victims by murdering them, and thereby maximizes well-being, what he does is impermissible. People have a right to self-determination, especially on matters of great importance such as whether to continue to live.

The welfarist need not give up just yet. Here are two possible responses. First, we might try to explain why we make the judgments we make about fairness, keeping promises, and respecting autonomy by appealing to the fact that when we all are disposed to make these sorts of judgments, the general welfare is promoted (Eggleston 2010). The judgments are false, but we have other welfare-based justifications for making them. This is a clever strategy, but you may find it difficult to believe that your judgments about the moral importance of fairness and such are mistaken.

Second, we might agree with the judgments, but appeal to welfare in a more indirect way to explain why they are true. Even though in some particular cases it might promote welfare to break a promise or violate autonomy, we are better-off in general if everyone keeps their promises and if we have conventions allowing for self-determination. The *rule utilitarian* attempts to explain the wrongness of harming one person to benefit others, breaking promises, and violating autonomy by appeal to facts about how well-off we would be if we didn't have rules against such things. Rather than evaluating an action by its effects on the total well-being, we evaluate an action by whether it conforms to a rule whose widespread adoption would have good effects on the total well-being. So the criterion of moral permissibility would be as follows:

> RU: An act is morally permissible if it conforms to a rule whose widespread adoption would have good effects on the total well-being.[12]

RU has been noted to have some problems. For instance, it sometimes seems that even though some rule would have

[12] See Hooker (2000) for a recent detailed defense of a version of rule utilitarianism. Hooker is not, however, a welfarist.

good effects on well-being if it were widely adopted, given that it is not widely adopted, one should not follow it. For example, suppose that studies showed that there are fewer accidents in countries where people drive on the left, and therefore people are better-off in those countries. You still shouldn't drive on the left if you are in a country where everyone else is driving on the right. The fact that we would be better-off if everyone drove on the left is irrelevant to what you should do when you go to your car. But since our concern is welfarism, let us ignore these sorts of complications.

RU seems unlikely to account fully for the importance of non-welfare components of morality. Consider a society that consists of a large majority group and a small minority group, and suppose the majority dislikes the minority. Suppose the majority group can benefit by exploiting the minority group. Total well-being might be promoted if everyone follows a moral code that permits exploitation of and discrimination against members of the minority group, provided the minority group is small enough and the majority group benefits sufficiently from the exploitation. So the moral importance of justice or fairness cannot be fully accounted for by RU. We must still assign fundamental importance to fair distribution. If so, welfarism is not true.

Welfarism is an extreme view, but its falsity does not mean that well-being is not of central importance. Well-being may play an important role in moral and political theory even if it is not the *only* thing that matters. Most obviously, the fact that an action makes people better-off is an important point in its favor when evaluating its moral status, and the fact that an act makes people worse off counts against it, even if not decisively. But that is not the only way in which well-being may be relevant. In the next two sections I will discuss other possible roles for well-being.

7.2   Well-Being, Harm, and Deontological Ethics

Utilitarian (or "consequentialist") moral theories are often contrasted with *deontological* theories of morality. There are many sorts of deontological principles. Here are two that are widely discussed:

> **The Doctrine of Doing and Allowing (DDA):** it is worse to do harm than to allow harm.
>
> **The Doctrine of Double Effect (DDE):** it is worse to harm someone as a means to achieving some good end than it is to harm someone as a merely foreseen side effect of achieving a good end.

DDA would explain why we think it is terribly wrong to murder someone, but not terribly wrong to fail to donate some money to a charity when doing so would save someone's life. Murder is doing harm; failing to donate is allowing harm. DDA is thus incompatible with utilitarianism, since according to utilitarianism all that matters are the effects of your alternatives on the total well-being, not whether those effects are due to "doing" something or "allowing" it to happen. DDE would explain why we can redirect a harm from a large group of people to one person, but cannot kill the one in order to use his organs to save the lives of the people in the larger group. Utilitarianism sees no important difference between what one brings about as a means and what one brings about as a side effect, since all that matters is what is brought about, so DDE is incompatible with utilitarianism.

DDA and DDE both utilize the notion of *harm*. Harm is naturally understood in terms of well-being. To harm someone, on a standard way of thinking about harm, is to make that person *worse off* than she would have otherwise been. If something doesn't make any difference to someone's welfare, why would we think it was harmful? So well-being may be almost as important for deontological ethics as it is for utilitarianism.

There are some cases that seem like cases of harm but where nobody is made worse off than they would have been. If two assassins independently put poison in their victim's drink, and each puts in an amount sufficient to kill the victim, then neither one of them does something that makes the victim worse off than he would have been otherwise; if the first assassin hadn't put in the poison, the victim would still have died in the same way due to the second assassin's poison, and the same is true of the second assassin given the presence of the first.

But these sorts of cases do not challenge the idea that well-being is closely linked to harm. Rather, they target the *counterfactual* component of the standard view of harm – the idea that *what would have happened* if an act had not been performed is relevant to whether that act is harmful. We might instead say that an act is harmful just in case it causes something bad to happen to someone; if this view were true, well-being and harm would still be connected. (This view also faces problems, since if someone is killed painlessly, nothing intrinsically bad happens to them, yet they are still harmed by being killed. But we need not explore these issues here.)

Other cases may give us reasons to doubt that harm and well-being are so tightly connected. In particular, there are some cases that seem like cases of harm that do not seem to involve a net loss of well-being.

> *Discrimination*: a racist airline refuses to sell a ticket to someone because of his race. The plane crashes killing all aboard. By refusing to sell the ticket, the airline saved the person's life. The customer is better-off in virtue of the discrimination, yet the discrimination still seems harmful. (See Woodward 1986: 810–11.)

> *Assault*: Nancy's enemy hits her in the knee with a baton, breaking her kneecap. While she is in the hospital for testing it is discovered that she has an aneurysm that would have killed her in a week. The doctors treat her and she is fully cured; had she not been attacked, she would have died, which would have been much worse for her. Yet the assault still harmed her. (See Woodward 1986: 809; Harman 2004: 99.)

> *Dentist*: A dentist sexually assaults his patients while they are under sedation. The patients never find out about it, and their conscious experience is never affected in any way by the assault. It seems they are not made worse off by the assault, yet the dentist still harmed the patients.

Perhaps, since there is no loss of well-being in these cases, it is a mistake to think of them as cases of harm. There is serious *wrongdoing* in each of these cases, and egregious violations of people's *rights*. But not all rights violations harm someone. For example, suppose you steal $100 from Bill Gates's wallet while he isn't looking. He has so much money that he never notices. He is no worse off for not having that money, but you have still violated his rights.

But Discrimination, Assault, and Dentist are much more serious cases of wrongdoing than stealing $100 from Bill Gates. When a rights violation fails to harm anyone, it typically seems like a fairly minor case of wrongdoing. Is it plausible to suppose that an act could be so seriously wrong without being a case of harm?

Perhaps these cases do involve harm. In Assault, Nancy is made better-off overall by the attack, but her well-being is at least temporarily, and in one way, lowered. So there may still be a connection between well-being and *pro tanto* harm, or harm in a respect. Nancy is harmed in a way, but not overall, given the later good effects of the attack. Dentist seems like a case where there is no loss of well-being only if we endorse a view of well-being like hedonism, according to which what you don't know can't hurt you. But if we assume the victim strongly wanted not to be assaulted, then there would be a loss of well-being in this case, too. So it is controversial whether these examples are problematic for the alleged connection between harm and well-being.

There may also be cases that are not harms but do involve a loss of well-being: one can make someone worse off than they would otherwise have been without harming them. For instance:

> *Gift*: I buy a gift for a friend and leave it on her doorstep. She would enjoy the gift if she got it. Then I change my mind and take the gift back before she ever knows anything about it. My friend is worse off than she would have been if I had not taken back the gift; but I have not harmed my friend.

> *Competition*: One company, merely as a result of making a better product, drives another company out of business. This makes the employees of the defunct company worse off. But the successful company has not harmed those employees.

Perhaps it is a mistake to think these are not cases of harm. Not all cases of harm are cases of wrongful action. You can harm your friend, and a company can harm rival companies' employees, without doing anything wrong. We just tend not to call an action harmful unless we mean to condemn it, and that's why we shrink from calling the actions in these cases harmful; but in fact they are harmful.

Recall, though, the reason we started thinking about the concept of harm in the first place: it is supposed to play an important role in deontological principles such as the Doctrine of Doing and Allowing and the Doctrine of Double Effect. These principles do not seem intended to apply to cases such as Gift and Competition. Suppose that, in Gift, I harm my friend by taking back the gift; now suppose that instead of taking back the gift, I simply choose not to buy a gift in the first place, thereby allowing my friend to be worse off than she would have been had I bought a gift. The Doctrine of Doing and Allowing seems to entail that I do something worse by taking back the gift (since this is doing harm) than I do by simply never buying a gift (since this is merely allowing harm). Friends of the DDA probably do not wish it to have this implication, which would indicate they would not wish to count what I do in Gift as harming my friend.

These considerations give us some reason to be skeptical that harm, when understood in terms of well-being, is well-suited to play a role in deontological theories. Of course, even if that is true, there are different conclusions we might draw. We might think deontological theories are false. Or we might think the notion of harm must be understood in a way that does not essentially involve effects on well-being.

7.3   Welfare Egalitarianism

Another role for well-being is in the theory of *distributive justice*. A theory of distributive justice tells us how to evaluate societies, or policies, or institutions with respect to the way they distribute goods. When resources are limited, society must make decisions about how to divide them up. There are many rules we might adopt: "finders keepers" and "keep whatever you are strong enough to hold onto" are rules that we sometimes end up following, but which do not seem particularly fair. Utilitarianism would tell us to divide things up in a way that maximizes well-being; but as we saw in section 7.1, maximizing well-being can lead to great unfairness, so utilitarianism is not a very plausible theory of distributive justice.

A more fair-sounding idea is that resources should be divided *equally*. But we might interpret this idea in different ways. We might think that to divide resources equally is just to give an equal amount of resources to each person; or we might instead think that to divide resources equally is to divide them in a way that makes people equally well-off. The former of these is called *resource egalitarianism*, and the latter is called *welfare egalitarianism*.

Here is an argument against resource egalitarianism (Arneson 1989). If we distribute an equal amount of money to each person, then we will give equal amounts of money to, say, an able-bodied person and a person who needs a wheelchair. The person who needs the wheelchair will then have to use a portion of her money on the wheelchair in order to live a flourishing life, and the able-bodied person will not. The able-bodied would gain an unfair advantage over the disabled. This suggests that resources should be distributed according to their effects on well-being, rather than simply in equal portions. We should distribute to the able-bodied and to the disabled a portion of resources that will enable them to flourish equally. What ultimately matters is one's welfare level, and the amount of resources you should get depends on how those resources will affect your welfare.

Another argument against resource egalitarianism is proposed by G.A. Cohen. Cohen argues that if someone is in pain, which can be relieved by some expensive pain medication, egalitarians should agree that he should get the medication. But this would be the case even if the pain did not result in any *loss of resources* for that person. Thus it is only by appealing to his well-being that the egalitarian can justify giving him the medicine (Cohen 1989: 919).

But welfare egalitarianism faces its own problems. Suppose it takes a lot of resources to make me happy in light of the fact that I have expensive tastes. If I am not going to the opera, driving a Porsche, and taking lavish vacations, I will be miserable. And suppose that it takes very little to make

George happy – he would be happy living in a small apartment with no car, some cheap books to read and ramen noodles to eat. Welfare egalitarianism seems to entail that it would be unjust for me to get the same amount of resources as George; justice would require me to get a much larger share of resources than George (on the assumption that enjoyment is what is intrinsically good for people). That hardly seems fair (Rawls 1971: 30–1; Cohen 1989: 912–13).

Welfare egalitarianism also has another, more practical difficulty in relation to resource egalitarianism. As we have seen, there are many different theories of welfare, and there is not widespread agreement about which theory is correct. There is much more agreement that, for example, it is good to have money, clothing, and shelter, than that, say, hedonism is true. This creates a practical difficulty in evaluating policies by a welfare egalitarian standard, since a policy might seem more just when evaluated according to one theory of well-being but more unjust according to another. This would happen if, for example, the policy would result in equality of hedonic levels but inequality of knowledge or achievement (White 2007: 83).

Here I am just scratching the tip of the iceberg. There are many moves for the egalitarian to make here. For instance, egalitarians might avoid some of the problems just noted by emphasizing the importance of equal *opportunity* for welfare, rather than equal welfare (Arneson 1989). The person with expensive tastes, for example, might have as equal an opportunity for welfare as the person with less expensive tastes, but simply fail to take advantage of that opportunity due to maintaining those expensive tastes. The debate between resource and welfare egalitarianism remains lively.

7.4 Asymmetries

We have moral reasons to benefit other people, and not to harm other people. But how strong are these reasons? Utilitarianism presupposes that positive and negative well-being provide reasons of equal but opposite strength. But it seems plausible to think that reasons not to harm people are stronger than reasons to benefit people. Let's suppose for the sake of argument that hedonism is true, and in particular that pleasures and pains can be weighed against one another, so that the value of one dolor of pain and one hedon of pleasure cancel each other out – a hedon and a dolor are equal but opposite in value. Now compare how we think about people bringing about, or not bringing about, some pleasures and pains. It seems positively required not to bring about pain in others, other things being equal. One who intentionally and gratuitously causes 10 dolors of pain in another is acting wrongly and deserves moral condemnation. But one who refrains from bringing about 10 hedons of pleasure in another person is not acting wrongly and should not be condemned for this failure. We might also put the point in this way: it is morally *required* to *refrain* from bringing about pain in others gratuitously, but it is not, in general, morally required to bring about pleasure in others. If this is all correct, then it seems that negative well-being generates *stronger reasons* than positive well-being. (In fact, a "negative utilitarian" thinks that our *only* moral obligation is to minimize negative well-being (Popper 1966: 284n); positive well-being is irrelevant to what we morally ought to do.) Or, perhaps, positive and negative well-being generate different kinds of reasons. We have reasons to bring about positive well-being, but not requiring reasons: it would be better if we brought about positive well-being, but we don't have to do it. But negative well-being generates requiring reasons: we are required not to create negative well-being unless there are sufficiently strong countervailing reasons (Dancy 2004: 24).

While this thought has some initial plausibility, it has problematic implications. Suppose I have the option of either bringing about no pleasure or pain for myself, or bringing about 11 hedons and 10 dolors. It makes sense for me to bring about the hedons and dolors – this would make me better-off, on the whole. But if negative well-being generates stronger reasons than positive well-being, then it is presumably possible for 10 dolors to generate stronger reasons than 11 hedons, in which case it seems I should have more reason not to take that combination of pleasure and pain. This seems wrong, even if sometimes we irrationally choose to forgo some benefits in order to avoid some less important pains.

Perhaps the reasons generated by the positive and negative well-being are different when they are produced in the agent of the act than when they are produced in others. So in the situation described in the previous paragraph, the hedons generate stronger reasons than the dolors only because I would be the one receiving them. But this can't quite be right. If I correctly want 11 hedons and 10 dolors, but can't bring them about for myself, why can't someone else do it for me?

It is more plausible that *autonomy* is playing some role here. Someone can bring about 11 hedons and 10 dolors for me, if I ask them to do so or if I consent to their doing so. But they can't bring about dolors in me without my consent. We have a right against others that they not cause us pain without permission. We do not have a corresponding right that they bring about some pleasure in us. (Or perhaps they do have a right, but it is merely a "positive right" rather than a "negative right," and negative rights are more stringent.) If this is the correct explanation of the difference in our obligations, then perhaps there is no asymmetry in the reason-giving force of pleasure and pain.

Related asymmetries may arise when considering our procreative choices. For example, it seems there is strong reason not to create someone who we know will be badly off. But there is no correspondingly strong reason to create someone who we know will be well-off. This suggests once again that negative well-being has stronger reason-generating force than positive well-being, at least in some instances. It also seems that if we have a choice between creating a new person with some positive well-being (without making any existing people worse off) or increasing the well-being level of an already-existing person, we should make the already-existing person better-off. But the same does not seem true concerning negative well-being; it seems just about equally bad to make an existing person worse off as to create a new person who will be badly off. So there again seems to be an asymmetry between positive and negative well-being: reasons against bringing about negative well-being are equally strong whether they involve already-existing people or not, while reasons to bring about positive well-being depend for their strength on whether the person already exists.

However, the idea that we do not have reason to create a happy person has been criticized. To take the simplest case, consider the view that given a choice between creating a well-off person or creating nobody, we would have no reason to create the person rather than not. According to this view, if we have a choice between creating someone with welfare of +10 or not creating that person, we have no reason to prefer either choice. Likewise if our choice were between creating someone with welfare of +20 or not creating that person. Now suppose we have a choice between creating someone with a well-being level of +10 or creating someone with a well-being level of +20. Since we have equal reason to create someone with welfare +10 as to create nobody, and we have equal reason to create nobody as to create someone with welfare +20, we must therefore (by the transitivity of equality) have equal reason to create someone with welfare +10 as to create someone with welfare +20. And that cannot be true (Broome 2004: 146–9). The alleged asymmetry between positive and negative welfare in procreation is not easy to defend.

7.5 Well-Being and Death

An interesting puzzle about well-being arises when we think about the harm of death. One perennial question about death is whether it is harmful to the one who dies. Let us first assume that there is no afterlife. If you survive your death, then whether your death will harm you depends on whether you will have a good afterlife or a bad one. But if there is no afterlife, then death will not harm you by causing bad things to happen to you. So is death harmful, if there is no afterlife?

It may seem that the answer is that it obviously is harmful. That's why killing people is so terribly wrong: it inflicts one of the greatest harms that one can inflict. But given that there is no afterlife, when you die you will just be a corpse, unable to have any sensations; or perhaps you would not exist at all. There doesn't seem to be anything inherently bad about that.

For instance, you'd experience no pain, you'd have no desires to frustrate, and you'd have no false beliefs. Epicurus appealed to such facts to argue that death is actually not harmful. His argument is based on what has been called the "problem of the subject" or the "timing problem":

> Death, the most dreaded of evils, is therefore of no concern to us; for while we exist death is not present, and when death is present we no longer exist. It is therefore nothing either to the living or to the dead since it is not present to the living, and the dead no longer are. (1964: 54)

The argument seems to be that death is bad for someone only if it is bad for her at some time, and there is no time at which death could be bad for anyone. It cannot be bad for you before you die, because you haven't died yet; it can't be bad for you once you die, because you stop existing at that point, and nothing can be bad for someone who does not exist. If you do not exist, then you cannot experience any pain. So death is not bad for you.

Epicurus was a hedonist; he thought that the only thing that is intrinsically bad for someone is pain. We could defend the badness of death by rejecting hedonism. Maybe there are things that are bad for you that, unlike pain, can happen to you after you have ceased to exist. Maybe a corpse could be said to be failing to develop essential human capacities, so that it is actually intrinsically bad to be a corpse. Or maybe the desires you had while alive would be frustrated by your death. But it seems strange to think that a hedonist would be unable to say that death is bad for its victim. The natural thing for the hedonist to say is that death is bad because it *deprives* the victim of pleasure. Thus death is not intrinsically bad. Rather it is instrumentally bad: it is bad in virtue of what it causes – or, in this case, what it prevents – for its victim.

But this still leaves open Epicurus's question: *when* does death harm its victim? That is, when is it the case that the person who dies is worse off than she would otherwise have been, had she not died then? All answers still seem to be ruled out. She was not worse off before she died – after all, she had not died yet! From the moment of death onward she does not exist, so it would seem she cannot be worse off at those times either.

Perhaps, though, the hedonist could argue that the victim is worse off after death than she would otherwise have been, as long as she would have been enjoying life. Since she doesn't exist while dead, she gets no pleasure or pain at those times, so it seems natural to say that, since nothing good or bad happens to her after death, her well-being level is stuck at zero – the neutral point between good and bad. If she would have been enjoying life had she not died, then her death is bad for her at those times when she would have been enjoying herself, since her well-being level would have been greater than zero (Bradley 2009: 88–92).

Some have argued, however, that this does not make sense: it is nonsensical to attribute any well-being level at all, even zero, to someone at a time at which they do not exist. This would be like attributing zero temperature to a nonexistent thing. If something does not exist at a time, it doesn't have zero temperature – it has no temperature at all! This raises a difficult question: whether well-being and temperature are really similar. Perhaps the hedonist could argue that unlike temperature, well-being can be attributed to someone at a time at which she does not exist. There are some properties, like *being eulogized*, that we often attribute to people at times after they have ceased to exist.

Another response is to reject the question of when death harms its victim. Some things can be bad for us even if they are not bad at any time – they are *atemporal* evils. Pleasures and pains are good or bad for us when they occur, but evils of deprivation, such as death, are not. Atemporal evils make you worse off without making you worse off at any time. Death makes you worse off by making your whole life go worse than it would otherwise have gone; it does this by preventing you from having extra goods in life, and we need say nothing more about *when* you are worse off (Broome 2012; Johansson 2012). John Broome gives the following analogy: suppose some words are cut from the end of a book. To determine how many words are cut from the book, you just compare the total number of words it has with the number it would have had; you don't look at which pages would have had more words on them. Likewise, he says, to determine how bad death is, you don't look at how much worse things are for the victim at particular times; you just look at the difference in total well-being between the actual and counterfactual lives. There is no time at which death harms its victim just as there is no page that is missing words (Broome 2012: 221–2).

Yet another response is to say that death harms you *before* you die. How could it do this? If hedonism is true, it would be impossible. But suppose a desire fulfillment view were true. Then we could say that death harms you by frustrating your desires, and the times at which it harms you are the times at which you have those desires – which of course is while you are still alive (Pitcher 1993). This doesn't mean that there is "backwards causation." Things happening after you die won't cause things to happen while you were still alive. Rather, they will make it the case that your desires were or were not fulfilled, unbeknownst to you.

The problem with this view, though, is that in cases not involving death, it seems wrong to say that we are benefited or harmed by a desire fulfillment or frustration at the time we had the desire. If I now want to go to a concert tomorrow, I am not *already* benefiting from the fact that I will go. So why should it be different in the case of death?

The harm of death raises difficult questions about well-being; so does the possibility of *posthumous* harm. It is natural to think that if someone was engaged in an important project but died just before its completion, we could benefit her by completing it for her or harm her by preventing its completion. But again, this thought presents puzzles. When would she be benefited by our completing her project? Could it be at the time we complete the project? This is a natural thought, but it would require us to say that she is well-off, has a positive well-being level, at times after she has died and no longer exists. This seems even more implausible than saying that she has a zero well-being level at those times. So she must be benefited before she died, if at any time – but again, it seems wrong to say that when a desire is fulfilled, the desirer is benefited at the time she has the desire rather than at the time of fulfillment. This suggests that the best solution for the believer in posthumous harm is to say that posthumous harm is *atemporally* bad for the one who is harmed.

But this is still not an entirely satisfactory notion, because when someone has a desire fulfilled or frustrated *while alive*, we do not think that the benefit or harm is atemporal; why should death be different? Why would some desire frustrations, but not others, affect how well-off you are at a time?

7.6 Further Reading

Mill's *Utilitarianism* (1861) and Book IV of Sidgwick's *The Methods of Ethics* (1907) contain classic defenses of utilitarianism. Chapter II of Ross's *The Right and the Good* (1988) contains important anti-utilitarian arguments. Also see David Lyons's *Forms and Limits of Utilitarianism* (1965) and J.J.C. Smart and Bernard Williams's *utilitarianism: For and Against* (1973). For defenses of rule utilitarianism, see Richard Brandt's *A Theory of the Good and the Right* (1979) and Brad Hooker's *Ideal Code, Real World* (2000). See Simon Keller's "Welfarism" (2009) for a good overview of welfarism and its problems. On welfare egalitarianism, see G.A. Cohen's "On the Currency of Egalitarian Justice" (1989) and Richard Arneson's "Equality and Equal Opportunity for Welfare" (1989). Elizabeth Anderson gives an important critique of Cohen's egalitarianism in "What is the Point of Equality?" (1999). On the nature of harm, Joel Feinberg's *Harm to Others* (1984) is a good place to start; see Bradley (2012) for a recent discussion of various accounts of harm. For an excellent collection of essays on asymmetries between harming and benefiting, in particular when it comes to creating people, see Melinda Roberts and David Wasserman (eds.), *Harming Future Persons* (2009). John Broome's *Weighing Lives* (2004) is another important recent contribution to debates about the ethics of creating people. For an argument similar to Broome's argument in section 7.4, that does not rely on transitivity, see my 2013, pp. 41–2. On the deprivation account of the evil of death, see Fred Feldman's *Confrontations with the Reaper* (1992), Bradley (2009), and several of the classic essays in John Fischer's *The Metaphysics of Death* (1993). On posthumous harms, see Steven Luper's "Retroactive Harms and Wrongs" (2012).

8
Conclusion

As we saw in the first several chapters of this book, there is no consensus about which theory of well-being is correct. I would like to close this book by suggesting that hedonism is, in important respects, to be preferred over alternative theories. The case I will make is of course only tentative, and readers with different philosophical inclinations will find other considerations more telling.

The main counterexample to hedonism, which has been thought to be the nail in hedonism's coffin, is the case of the experience machine (and of false pleasures in general). If we are to be persuaded by the experience machine example to think that hedonism is false, it must be because we think that an appropriate connection to the outside world is an essential part of well-being. Perhaps the connection involves being accurately informed about what is happening in the world; or perhaps it involves shaping the world to fit your desires. In either case, things happening outside of you will be essential to determining your well-being – not merely by *causing* you to be happy, as the hedonist thinks, but by being *components* of your well-being.

The problem is that once we allow things outside of you to be components of your well-being, and allow your well-being to fluctuate independently of what is going on inside you or in your mind, strange consequences follow. The strange consequences are particularly salient when we think about what it is to be doing well or badly *at a time*. Think about some times in the past when you have had a good day, or a bad week. What made it the case that you had a good day? It was probably something that happened that day. But suppose that a desire fulfillment view is true; then what made it the case that you had a good day might be something that happened on some other day (Bradley 2009). And this is strange; it seems wrong to say that you had a good day on Tuesday because on Friday something happened that you wanted. In that case, it would make more sense to say that Friday was a good day for you. We can bring out the oddness here by imagining that you die on Wednesday. If something would directly affect your well-being, for example because it is something you desire to happen, and it happens after you die, it seems that it could make you well-off at a time at which you are dead. And why not, if we are rejecting the idea that well-being is an internal mental state of yours?

Hedonism has no such implications. A good day for you is a day during which you are pleased more than pained. Nothing happening on any other day is relevant to whether you are pleased today. I think this is an underappreciated advantage of hedonism. It is underappreciated because philosophers tend to focus on whether someone's whole life goes well for her, rather than on how things go for someone at a moment or during a single day or week. Some philosophers find nothing odd about saying that whether someone's whole life went well or badly depends on things that happened after the person died; but in that case they should also find nothing odd about saying that whether someone had a good or bad day depends on what happened on some later day.

The hedonist still has an explanatory burden. Most people think that some things other than pleasure are components of well-being: friendship, desire fulfillment, developing one's capacities, knowledge, meaningfulness, freedom...there may be disagreement about which of these things are good, but most of us think that at least some of these things are good. The hedonist owes us some explanation of why we think any of these things are good for us in themselves.

Fortunately, the hedonist has such an explanation: it makes us happy to believe that these other things are good. When we think something is good, we tend to pursue it. Pursuing friendship and knowledge is an effective way to be happy. At least, it is better than directly pursuing happiness, by trying to predict what will make us happy and then pursuing that thing. This way of thinking about the good life is well expressed by J.S. Mill in his *Autobiography*:

> I never, indeed, wavered in the conviction that happiness is the test of all rules of conduct, and the end of life. But I now thought that this end was only to be attained by not making it the direct end. Those only are happy (I thought) who have their minds fixed on some object other than their own happiness; on the happiness of others, on the improvement of mankind, even on some art or pursuit, followed not as a means, but as itself an ideal end. Aiming thus at something else, they find happiness by the way...The only chance is to treat, not happiness, but some end external to it, as the purpose of life. (1861: 88)

Mill's assertion is an empirical claim. But it seems plausible, and in fact I think that some of the social science research on subjective well-being gives us reason to think Mill was right. As we saw in chapter 6, we are often not very good at predicting what sorts of things will make us happy. We think losing a limb would devastate us, but in the long term it probably wouldn't. We think winning the lottery would make us happy, but it probably wouldn't. Thus if we use our own predicted happiness as a basis for decision-making, we will probably make mistakes, and will do worse for ourselves than if we focus on cultivating friendships and pursuing knowledge.

The fact that we are happier if we do not directly pursue happiness has been called the "paradox of hedonism." This is not exactly a paradox. Rather, hedonism is what Parfit calls a "self-effacing" theory (1984: ch. 1). It tells us that pleasure is good for us, but – when combined with the claim that we prudentially ought to pursue whatever will result in us being better-off if we pursue it – it also tells us *not to pursue* pleasure, because pursuing pleasure is a worse way to get pleasure than pursuing other things.

Thus hedonism offers a kind of justification of our judgments that things such as knowledge and friendship are valuable in themselves for us. Even though those judgments are false, we should keep believing them because by doing so, we more effectively pursue pleasure, which is what is really good for us. Thus it is important to distinguish between two claims:

H: Pleasure is the only thing that is intrinsically good.
H*: Pleasure is the only thing that it is prudent to pursue for its own sake.

The hedonist thinks H is true but H* is false. Conversely:

K: Knowledge is intrinsically good.
K*: It is prudent to pursue knowledge for its own sake.

The hedonist thinks K* is true (or may be true) but K is false. So the hedonist can explain why someone would, and perhaps should, think that hedonism is false: on hedonistic grounds, it is prudent to value things other than pleasure for themselves.[13]

This explanation creates awkwardness. For it seems that while thinking abstractly about well-being and trying to have true beliefs about what is good for us, we should believe hedonism. But while living our lives we are generally better-off forgetting about hedonism, and in fact should probably act as if it is false. This is an awkwardness that we may just have to accept.[14]

Whether you are willing to accept this story may depend on your general philosophical temperament. Some philosophers are generally unwilling to overturn a judgment on theoretical grounds – in this case, to abandon the judgment that knowledge or friendship is valuable in itself in order to endorse a general theory of well-being. Others are more willing to accept that our pre-theoretical judgments must be abandoned in order to achieve sufficient theoretical unity. I find myself in the latter category: I find that pluralistic theories do not offer enough unity to offer satisfying explanations.

---

[13] This is an application of what Ben Eggleston (2010) calls the method of "practical equilibrium" to the case of hedonism.
[14] Perhaps this is to say that hedonism is a "schizophrenic" theory in Michael Stocker's sense (Stocker 1976).

And since I also think that perfectionist theories presuppose unacceptable theories of human nature, and that desire fulfillment theories cannot account for well-being at a time, I am left with hedonism as the only unified theory with sufficient plausibility.

If I am right to conclude that hedonism is the correct theory of well-being, then it turns out that social scientists have largely been on the right track in their investigations of subjective well-being. But it is worth emphasizing that hedonism remains a minority position among philosophers of well-being, and that nobody should be overly confident that their preferred theory is correct. Social scientists would do well to take alternative views seriously as well, and measure the kinds of things to which those views attribute value. In any case, scientific work on well-being will be well served by greater awareness on the part of scientists of the underlying assumptions their work makes about well-being, and the corresponding limits these assumptions place on that work.

A final note of caution (or for some, optimism): the case I have made for hedonism raises questions that philosophers of well-being have only just begun to think about. Hardly anyone has written about what it is to have a good day; the focus has been almost exclusively on whole lives. If philosophers focus attention on these questions about shorter spans of time, it is possible that other views might be found to offer plausible explanations of what it is to have a good day.

References

Adams, Robert. (1999) *Finite and Infinite Goods*. Oxford University Press.

Alexandrova, Anna. (2011) "Values and the Science of Well-being." In Harold Kincaid (ed.), *The Oxford Handbook of Philosophy of Social Science* (Oxford University Press), pp. 625–45.

Alexandrova, Anna. (2012) "Well-Being as an Object of Science." *Philosophy of Science* 79: 678–89.

Anderson, Elizabeth. (1999) "What is the Point of Equality?" *Ethics* 109: 287–337.

Annas, Julia. (1998) "Virtue and Eudaimonism." *Social Philosophy and Policy* 15: 37–55.

Aristotle. (1976) *Nicomachean Ethics*, trans. J.A.K. Thomson. Penguin Books.

Arneson, Richard. (1989) "Equality and Equal Opportunity for Welfare." *Philosophical Studies* 56: 77–93.

Benatar, David. (2006) *Better Never to Have Been: The Harm of Coming into Existence*. Oxford University Press.

Bentham, Jeremy. (1962 [1789]) "Introduction to the Principles of Morals and Legislation (Chapters I–V)." In Mary Warnock (ed.), *John Stuart Mill: Utilitarianism, On Liberty, Essay on Bentham, together with selected writings of Jeremy Bentham and John Austin* (Meridian), pp. 33–77.

Bloomfield, Paul. (2014) *The Virtues of Happiness*. Oxford University Press.

Bradford, Gwen. (2013) "The Value of Achievements." *Pacific Philosophical Quarterly* 94: 204–24.

Bradley, Ben. (2009) *Well-Being and Death*. Oxford University Press.

Bradley, Ben. (2010) "Benatar and the Logic of Betterness," *Journal of Ethics and Social Philosophy*, March, www.jesp.org.

Bradley, Ben. (2012) "Doing Away With Harm." *Philosophy and Phenomenological Research* 85: 390–412.

Bradley, Ben. (2013) "Asymmetries in Benefiting, Harming and Creating." *The Journal of Ethics* 17: 37–49.

Brandt, Richard. (1979) *A Theory of the Good and the Right*. Oxford University Press.

Brentano, Franz. (1902 [1889]) *The Origin of Our Knowledge of Right and Wrong*. Archibald Constable & Co.

Brentano, Franz. (2009 [1952]) *The Foundation and Construction of Ethics*, trans. E. Schneewind. Routledge.

Brickman, Phillip, Dan Coates, and Ronnie Janoff-Bulman. (1978). "Lottery Winners and Accident Victims: Is Happiness Relative?" *Journal of Personality and Social Psychology* 36: 917–27.

Broome, John. (2004) *Weighing Lives*. Oxford University Press.

Broome, John. (2012) "The Badness of Death and the Goodness of Life." In Ben Bradley, Fred Feldman and Jens Johansson (eds.), *Oxford Handbook of Philosophy of Death*, Oxford University Press, pp. 218–33.

Carson, Thomas. (2000) *Value and the Good Life*. University of Notre Dame Press.

Chang, Ruth (ed.) (1998) *Incommensurability, Incomparability, and Practical Reason*. Harvard University Press.

Chisholm, Roderick. (1986) *Brentano and Intrinsic Value*. Cambridge University Press.

Cohen, G.A. (1989) "On the Currency of Egalitarian Justice." *Ethics* 99: 906–44.

Crisp, Roger. (2006) *Reasons and the Good*. Oxford University Press.

Crisp, Roger. (2013) "Well-Being." In Edward N. Zalta (ed.), *The Stanford Encyclopedia of Philosophy* (Summer 2013 Edition). Available at: http://plato.stanford.edu/archives/sum2013/entries/well-being/.

Dancy, Jonathan. (2004) *Ethics Without Principles*. Oxford University Press.

Darwall, Stephen. (2004) *Welfare and Rational Care*. Princeton University Press.

Davis, Wayne. (1981) "Pleasure and Happiness." *Philosophical Studies* 39: 305–17.

Diener, Ed and Richard Lucas. (1999) "Personality and Subjective Well-Being." In Daniel Kahneman, Ed Diener, and

Norbert Schwarz (eds.), *Well-Being*, Russell Sage Foundation, pp. 213–29.

Diener, Ed, Derrick Wirtz and Shigehiro Oishi. (2001) "End Effects of Rated Life Quality: The James Dean Effect." *Psychological Science* 12: 124–8.

Dorsey, Dale. (2010) "Three Arguments for Perfectionism." *Nous* 44: 59–79.

Dorsey, Dale. (2012) "Intrinsic Value and the Supervenience Principle." *Philosophical Studies* 157: 267–85.

Eggleston, Ben. (2010) "Practical Equilibrium: A Way of Deciding What to Think about Morality." *Mind* 119: 549–74.

Epicurus. (1964) *Letters, Principal Doctrines, and Vatican Sayings*, trans. Russel Geer. Bobbs-Merrill.

Feinberg, Joel. (1984) *Harm to Others*. Oxford University Press.

Feldman, Fred. (1992) *Confrontations with the Reaper*. Oxford University Press.

Feldman, Fred. (1995) "Justice, Desert, and the Repugnant Conclusion." *Utilitas* 7: 189–206.

Feldman, Fred. (2004) *Pleasure and the Good Life*. Oxford University Press.

Feldman, Fred. (2010) *What Is This Thing Called Happiness?* Oxford University Press.

Finnis, John. (2011) *Natural Law and Natural Rights*, 2nd edn. Oxford University Press.

Fischer, John (ed.). (1993) *The Metaphysics of Death*. Stanford University Press.

Foot, Philippa. (2001) *Natural Goodness*. Oxford University Press.

Frederick, Shane and George Loewenstein. (1999) "Hedonic Adaptation." In Daniel Kahneman, Ed Diener, and Norbert Schwarz (eds.), *Well-Being*, Russell Sage Foundation, pp. 302–29.

Glasgow, Joshua. (2013) "The Shape of a Life and the Value of Loss and Gain." *Philosophical Studies* 162: 665–82.

Griffin, James. (1986) *Well-Being*. Oxford University Press.

Harman, Elizabeth. (2004) "Can We Harm and Benefit in Creating?" *Philosophical Perspectives* 18: 89–113.

Hawkins, Jennifer. (2006) "Well-Being, Autonomy, and the Horizon Problem." *Utilitas* 20: 143–68.

Haybron, Dan. (2001) "Happiness and Pleasure." *Philosophy and Phenomenological Research* 62: 501–28.

Haybron, Dan. (2008) *The Pursuit of Unhappiness*. Oxford University Press.

Heathwood, Chris. (2005) "The Problem of Defective Desires." *Australasian Journal of Philosophy* 83: 487–504.

Heathwood, Chris. (2007) "The Reduction of Sensory Pleasure to Desire." *Philosophical Studies* 133: 23–44.

Hooker, Brad. (1996) "Does Moral Virtue Constitute a Benefit to the Agent?" In Roger Crisp (ed.), *How Should One Live? Essays on the Virtues*, Oxford University Press, pp. 141–56.

Hooker, Brad. (2000) *Ideal Code, Real World*. Oxford University Press.

Hurka, Thomas. (1993) *Perfectionism*. Oxford University Press.

Hurka, Thomas. (2011) *The Good Things in Life*. Oxford University Press.

Hursthouse, Rosalind. (1999) *On Virtue Ethics*. Oxford University Press.

Johansson, Jens. (2012) "The Timing Problem." In Ben Bradley, Fred Feldman and Jens Johansson (eds.), *Oxford Handbook of Philosophy of Death*, Oxford University Press, pp. 255–73.

Kahneman, Daniel. (1999). "Objective Happiness." In Daniel Kahneman, Ed Diener, and Norbert Schwarz (eds.), *Well-Being*, Russell Sage Foundation, pp. 3–25.

Kahneman, Daniel, Ed Diener, and Norbert Schwarz (eds.) (1999) *Well-Being: The Foundations of Hedonic Psychology*. Russell Sage Foundation.

Kawall, Jason. (1999) "The Experience Machine and Mental State Theories of Well-Being." *The Journal of Value Inquiry* 33: 381–7.

Kazez, Jean. (2007) *The Weight of Things: Philosophy and the Good Life*. Blackwell Publishing.

Keller, Simon. (2004) "Welfare and the Achievement of Goals." *Philosophical Studies* 121: 27–41.

Keller, Simon. (2009) "Welfarism." *Philosophy Compass* 4: 82–95.

Khader, Serene. (2011) *Adaptive Preferences and Women's Empowerment*. Oxford University Press.

Kitcher, Philip. (1999) "Essence and Perfection." *Ethics* 110: 59–83.

Kraut, Richard. (1994) "Desire and the Human Good." *Proceedings and Addresses of the American Philosophical Association* 68: 39–54.

Kraut, Richard. (2007) *What is Good and Why: The Ethics of Well-Being*. Harvard University Press.

LaPorte, Joseph. (1997) "Essential Membership." *Philosophy of Science* 64: 96–112.

Lewis, David. (1986) *On the Plurality of Worlds*. Blackwell Publishing.

Lewis, David. (1988) "Desire as Belief." *Mind* 97: 323–32.

Liebesman, David. (2011) "Simple Generics." *Nous* 45: 409–42.

Lucas, Richard and Nicole Lawless. (2013) "Does Life Seem Better on a Sunny Day? Examining the Association between Daily

Weather Conditions and Life Satisfaction Judgments." *Journal of Personality and Social Psychology* 104: 872–84.

Luhmann, Maike, Wilhelm Hofmann, Michael Eid, and Richard Lucas. (2012) "Subjective Well-Being and Adaptation to Life Events: A Meta-Analysis on Differences between Cognitive and Affective Well-Being." *Journal of Personality and Social Psychology* 102: 592–615.

Luper, Steven. (2012) "Retroactive Harms and Wrongs." In Ben Bradley, Fred Feldman and Jens Johansson (eds.), *Oxford Handbook of Philosophy of Death*, Oxford University Press, pp. 317–35.

Lyons, David. (1965) *Forms and Limits of Utilitarianism*. Oxford University Press.

McDaniel, Kris. (2014) "A Moorean View of the Value of Lives." *Pacific Philosophical Quarterly* 95: 23–46.

Metz, Thaddeus. (2013) *Meaning in Life*. Oxford University Press.

Mill, J.S. (1861) *Utilitarianism*. Republished in 1957 by Macmillan.

Mill, J.S. (1961) *Essential Works of John Stuart Mill*, ed. Max Lerner. Bantam Books.

Moore, G.E. (1903) *Principia Ethica*. Cambridge University Press.

Nagel, Thomas. (1986) *The View from Nowhere*. Oxford University Press.

Nagel, Thomas. (1993) "Death." In John Fischer (ed.), *The Metaphysics of Death*, Stanford University Press, pp. 61–9.

Nozick, Robert. (1974) *Anarchy, State and Utopia*. Basic Books.

Nussbaum, Martha. (2011) *Creating Capabilities: The Human Development Approach*. Harvard University Press.

Overvold, Mark. (1984) "Morality, Self-Interest, and Reasons for Being Moral." *Philosophy and Phenomenological Research* 44: 493–507.

Parfit, Derek. (1984) *Reasons and Persons*. Oxford University Press.

Parfit, Derek. (1986) "Overpopulation and the Quality of Life." In Peter Singer (ed.), *Applied Ethics*, Oxford University Press, pp. 145–64.

Pitcher, George. (1993) "The Misfortunes of the Dead." In John Fischer (ed.), *The Metaphysics of Death*, Stanford University Press, pp. 159–68.

Popper, Karl. (1966) *The Open Society and Its Enemies: The Spell of Plato*, vol. 1, 5th edn. Princeton University Press.

Railton, Peter. (2003) *Facts, Values, and Norms*. Cambridge University Press.

Rath, Tom and James Harter. (2010) *Wellbeing: The Five Essential Elements*. Gallup.

Rawls, John. (1971) *A Theory of Justice*. Harvard University Press.

Redelmeier, D.A. and Daniel Kahneman. (1996) "Patients' Memories of Painful Medical Treatments: Real-Time and Retrospective Evaluations of Two Minimally Invasive Procedures." *Pain* 66: 3–8.

Roberts, Melinda and David Wasserman (eds.). (2009) *Harming Future Persons: Ethics, Genetics and the Nonidentity Problem*. Springer.

Rosati, Connie. (1995) "Persons, Perspectives, and Full Information Accounts of the Good." *Ethics* 105: 296–325.

Rosati, Connie. (2006) "Personal Good." In Terry Horgan and Mark Timmons (eds.), *Metaethics after Moore*, Oxford University Press, pp. 107–32.

Ross, W.D. (1988) *The Right and the Good*. Hackett. (First published 1930 by Oxford University Press.)

Ryberg, Jesper and Torbjörn Tännsjö (eds.). (2004) *The Repugnant Conclusion*. Kluwer Academic.

Scanlon, T.M. (1998) *What We Owe to Each Other*. Harvard University Press.

Schwarz, Norbert and Gerald L. Clore. (1983) "Mood, Misattribution, and Judgments of Well-Being: Informative and Directive Functions of Affective States." *Journal of Personality and Social Psychology* 45: 513–23.

Sen, Amartya. (1999) *Commodities and Capabilities*. Oxford University Press.

Sidgwick, Henry. (1907) *The Methods of Ethics*, 7th edn. Hackett Publishing.

Smart, J.J.C. and Bernard Williams. (1973) *Utilitarianism: For and Against*. Cambridge University Press.

Smuts, Aaron. (2011) "The Feels Good Theory of Pleasure." *Philosophical Studies* 155: 241–65.

Sobel, David. (1994) "Full Information Accounts of Well-Being." *Ethics* 104: 784–810.

Stocker, Michael. (1976) "The Schizophrenia of Modern Ethical Theories." *The Journal of Philosophy* 73: 453–66.

Sumner, L.W. (1996) *Welfare, Happiness and Ethics*. Oxford University Press.

Tatarkiewicz, Wladyslaw. (1976) *Analysis of Happiness*. Martinus Nijhoff.

Taylor, Richard. (2004) "The Meaning of Life." In David Benatar (ed.), *Life, Death, and Meaning*, Rowman & Littlefield, pp. 19–28.

Taylor, Shelley and Jonathon Brown. (1988) "Illusion and Well-Being: A Social Psychological Perspective on Mental Health." *Psychological Bulletin* 103: 193–210.

Tiberius, Valerie. (2006) "Well-Being: Psychological Research for Philosophers." *Philosophy Compass* 1: 493–505.

Tiberius, Valerie. (2013) "Philosophical Methods in Happiness Research." In Susan David, Ilona Boniwell and Amanda Conley Ayers (eds.), *The Oxford Handbook of Happiness*, Oxford University Press, pp. 315–25.

Velleman, David. (1993) "Well-Being and Time." In John Fischer (ed.), *The Metaphysics of Death*, Stanford University Press, pp. 329–57.

White, Stuart. (2007) *Equality*. Polity.

Wolf, Susan. (2010) *Meaning in Life and Why it Matters*. Princeton University Press.

Woodward, James. (1986) "The Non-Identity Problem." *Ethics* 96: 804–31.

Yardley, John and Robert Rice. (1991) "The Relationship between Mood and Subjective Well-Being." *Social Indicators Research* 24: 101–11.

Index

CPSIA information can be obtained
at www.ICGtesting.com
Printed in the USA
JSHW042145010622
26485JS00006B/110

9 780745 662732